Martian in the Playground

Revised Edition

'This deceptively little book contains more truth and provides more insight into what it is like to have Asperger's Syndrome than many weighty tome on the subject. It offers a view from the inside, but it is not yet another autobiography. Admirably and refreshingly, the author has refrained from giving an account solely based on her own experiences. Instead she sets out observations from 25 different sufferers, giving often astonishing and sometimes harrowing glimpses of what actually happens to a child with Asperger's Syndrome in the classroom, in the playground, in the lunch queue and at home'.
The Journal of Child Psychology and Psychiatry

In her book *Martian in the Playground*, Clare Sainsbury gives a scholarly and insightful description of the experience of people with Asperger's Syndrome. The accounts of their memories of school, both in the classroom and in social settings, should be read by all involved in education of students with an autistic disorder. This book will be if interest to all who are involved with Asperger's Syndrome: parents, professional and the young people themselves
Dr Jane Shields, Director NAS EarlyBird Centre

This is amazingly informative book that should be read by every parent/family of a child with Asperger's Syndrome. It should also be included on the reading list of any teachers who have an Asperger's pupil in their class…. I am deeply grateful to Clare Sainsbury for writing this book because now when I am forced to justify my son's outrageous behaviour to members of my family, friends and acquaintances I can save my breadth and just hand them this wonderful volume
Grapevine

It is to be hoped that teachers and others who deal with children and young people in group settings will read this book and realize that there is a positive as well as a negative side to autism. Whilst it is a huge burden for any parents to know that their child is different, if must help to know that that child can be happy. In trying to help children conform to a fairly arbitrary 'norm', do we risk turning some with much to contribute, into misfits whose families and schools apologize for them rather than celebrating their very individual learning styles, personalities and potential?
Jane Lovey, University of Cambridge

Martian in the Playground

Understanding the Schoolchild with
Asperger's Syndrome

Revised Edition

Clare Sainsbury

Illustrations: Philippa Drakeford

Los Angeles | London | New Delhi
Singapore | Washington DC

This edition first published 2009
First edition published 2000 (reprinted 2003, 2004, 2006, 2008)

This edition reprinted 2010, 2012 (twice)

SAGE Publications
1 Oliver's Yard
55 City Road
London EC1Y 1SP

SAGE Publications Inc.
2455 Teller Road
Thousand Oaks, California 91320

SAGE Publications India Pvt Ltd
B 1/I 1 Mohan Cooperative Industrial Area
Mathura Road, Post Bag 7
New Delhi 110 044

SAGE Publications Asia-Pacific Pte Ltd
3 Church Street
#10-04 Samsung Hub
Singapore 049483

Library of Congress Control Number 2009923423

British Library Cataloguing in Publication data

A catalogue record for this book is available from the British Library

ISBN 978-1-84920-000-4 (pbk)

Typeset by C&M Digitals (P) Ltd, Chennai, India
Printed on paper from sustainable resources
Printed in Great Britain by the MPG Books Group

MIX
Paper from
responsible sources
FSC
www.fsc.org   FSC® C018575

Contents

Acknowledgements

I would like to thank:

All the other people with Asperger's syndrome who trusted me with their memories and opinions, often despite having never met me in person – I would thank them all by name if I could do so without breaching their anonymity; Gunilla Gerland; Jean-Paul Bovee; the members of Autuniv-l and InLv; Uta Frith and FrancescaHappé; the staff and students of Springhallow School; my parents, for sharing their memories of my school days, and for the support without which I would never have survived school in the first place; Kate Rowlatt; and finally the good teachers in my life, including Miss Rushforth, Miss O'Neill, Miss Lee, Miss Gough, Dr. Greenwood, and Jonathan Glover.

Martian in the Playground
was the winner of the Best Academic Book Award
National Association for Special Educational Needs
Times Educational Supplement
November 2000.

Foreword

This is an exceptional book. Its aim is to illuminate what it means to be a person who has Asperger syndrome, by providing a window into a unique and particular world. Drawing on her own experience of schooling, and that of a network of friends and correspondents who share her way of thinking and responding, Clare Sainsbury reminds us of the unique potential for harm whicheducation holds for those who do not "fit".

There are many memories in the book of bullying, of constantly being told off and never knowing why, of intolerance and lack of understanding from teachers and other children. It is not all bad news, however. There are also positive memories of teachers who were able to grasp the nature of the autistic experience, and create in their classrooms places of safety and intellectual challenge. This book tells us how this can be done successfully, when adults and peers have an understanding of the autistic person's inability to learn the rules of social interaction without explicit teaching, their literalness, their different distribution of focused attention, their lack of any self-protecting artifice.

On these and other issues this book holds insights which take us beyond the standard guidance on how to 'manage' autistic spectrum disorder. It challenges the way we might handle obsessional behaviour; it invites us to celebrate the 'pure passion of the intellect' which such obsessions can represent, and to recognise the delight which can be experienced by children who love to collect, catalogue and order. It reminds us that many of the autistic mannerisms we might try to suppress actually help the child to think. It explains what trying to focus attention feels like for autistic people and how teachers can work with this. It tells us about the pain of sensory hyper-sensitivity, and conjures up our own memories of school as noisy, chaotic places – only many times magnified for the person with autistic spectrum disorder.

All of this information Clare gives to us 'from the inside'. In doing this, she adds a new perspective to professional texts which are written 'from the outside', and which, however hard they try, always carry a message that something is 'wrong' with children with special educational needs. This book challenges that assumption. It invites us to recognise that people with Asperger syndrome are not malfunctioning curiosities who need to be fixed, but people who are simply different from ourselves – and often, as anyone who has worked extensively with people with autistic spectrum disorder will attest, rather nicer and more interesting than many people without such a 'disorder'. They are disabled only to the extent to which we have not yet succeeded in adapting the way we teach, and the way we organise the social environment of school, to their particular way of being. In a context where recent reports indicate as many as one in seventy three year olds are being diagnosed with autism or Asperger syndrome, and where every teacher at some point will have such a child in their classroom, it is essential that we get on with making these adaptations. This book will be invaluable in helping us to do so.

Jean Gross

Research in the Field of Asperger's Syndrome

There have always been children who have the unusual profile of abilities we describe as Asperger's syndrome. However, it is only in the last 25 years that we have had a diagnostic term to describe such children (Wing 1981). The diagnosis is based on the original descriptions of Dr Hans Asperger, a Viennese paediatrician, who, in the late 1930s, noticed that some of the children referred to his clinic had very similar personality characteristics, abilities and behaviour. He noted that their social maturity and social reasoning were conspicuously delayed, despite having intellectual abilities within the normal range. Some aspects of their social abilities, such as reduced eye contact, were quite unusual at any stage of development. The children sought friendship but had considerable difficulty making and keeping friends. Due to being different to other children and socially isolated, they were often teased and bullied. For some children, retaliation had led to suspension from school and a referral to his clinic. He also noted unusual aspects of verbal and non-verbal communication, especially the conversational aspects of language. While the syntax and vocabulary may have been relatively advanced, the child could be notoriously pedantic, tending to make literal interpretations; and some children had an unusual prosody that affected the tone, pitch and rhythm of speech. Asperger also described conspicuous difficulties with the communication and control of emotions, and empathy was not as mature as one would expect, considering the children's intellectual abilities. The children also had an intense fascination with a specific topic or interest that would dominate their thoughts and time. Asperger noted that teachers described the children as having difficulty maintaining attention in class and psychological assessments indicated specific learning problems. When talking to their parents, he noted that the children often needed more assistance with daily living and organizational skills than one would expect. He also observed movement problems in terms of clumsiness in gait and coordination, and some children were extremely sensitive to particular sounds, aromas, textures and touch. All of these abilities and behaviours are now recognised as characteristics associated with Asperger's syndrome.

Most children have the diagnosis confirmed during the primary school years (Eisenmajer et al. 1996; Howlin and Asgharian 1999), although some achieve a diagnosis in their teenage years. In the early school years, social play tends to be more action than conversation, with friendships being transitory and social games relatively simple with clear rules. In adolescence, friendships are based on more complex interpersonal rather than practical needs, someone to confide in rather than someone to play ball with. In the primary school years, the child has one teacher for the whole year and both teacher and child learn how to read each other's signals and develop a working relationship. There is also more guidance, flexibility and leniency with regard to the school curriculum and expected social and emotional maturity. Social and academic life is relatively simple and the child may be less aware of being different to other children, and his or her difficulties may not be conspicuous to teachers in the classroom or playground. However, the child may first realize that he or she is different to other children between the ages of six and eight years. Clare was about eight years old when she describes feeling different to other children (see p. 25).

During adolescence, a teenager with Asperger's syndrome is likely to become increasingly socially isolated, aware of being different to his or her peers and having conspicuous difficulty with the planning and organizational skills needed to complete assignments and homework on time. This can lead to a deterioration in school grades that comes to the attention of teachers and parents. The social isolation and resulting low self-esteem can lead to signs of a clinical depression, intense anxiety in social situations and concern regarding anger management when teased, confused or frustrated. Thus some children do not achieve a diagnosis until they are attending secondary or high school.

The majority of children referred for a diagnostic assessment for Asperger's syndrome are boys, with a ratio of about four boys to one girl (Attwood 2007). Girls with Asperger's syndrome may be more difficult to recognize and diagnose due to coping and camouflaging mechanisms, which can also be used by some boys. One of the coping mechanisms is to learn how to act in a social setting, as described by Liane Holliday Willey in her autobiography, *Pretending to be Normal* (Willey 1999). Girls can develop the ability to 'disappear' in a large group, being on the periphery of social interaction. They are 'on the outside looking in'. They may use strategies to avoid active participation in class proceedings, such as being well-behaved and polite, and apologising for social errors or faux pas; in this way, they may then be left alone by teachers and peers.

There are several diagnostic criteria used by clinicians to confirm a diagnosis. The general consensus among clinicians, confirmed by subsequent research, is that Asperger's syndrome occurs in about one child in 250 (Ehlers and Gillberg 1993; Kadesjo, Gillberg and Hagberg 1999). A school can estimate the number of children who will have the characteristics of Asperger's syndrome by dividing the number of children registered at the school by 250. Thus most schools will have at least one child diagnosed with Asperger's syndrome.

The education of children with Asperger's syndrome

The social curriculum

School is an educational and social environment. Children with Asperger's syndrome have difficulties with both these aspects of school. In typical children, the acquisition of social and especially friendship skills is based on an innate ability that develops throughout childhood in association with progressive changes in cognitive ability, and modified and matured through social experiences and guidance. Children with Asperger's syndrome are not able to rely on intuitive abilities in social settings as well as their peers and must rely more on their cognitive abilities, experiences and guidance from parents, teachers and peers. It is essential that children who have Asperger's syndrome receive tuition and guided practice in the ability to read and understand social situations as well as social cues, such as facial expressions. They also need to learn, rather than be expected to know, how to make and keep friends (Attwood 2000).

Parents can try to facilitate social understanding and successful interactive play at home with siblings or another child invited to their home on a play date, but will have difficulty providing the range of experiences and degree of supervision and tuition required for a child with Asperger's syndrome. The optimum environment to learn the social curriculum and develop reciprocal play with peers is at school. Schools will need to be aware of the importance of the social curriculum as well as an educational curriculum for a child with Asperger's syndrome. Fortunately, we now have resources to teach the social curriculum that have been specifically designed for children with Asperger's syndrome and can be implemented by teachers in the classroom and the playground (see the Appendix of Recommened Resources at the end of this chapter.).

Clare describes the difficulties she faced with integration with other children and mixing the academic and social curriculum (see p. 26). This is a typical experience of children with Asperger's syndrome, and teachers need to be aware of the confusion and stress of the social and academic worlds of school. Being in school is intellectually and emotionally exhausting as the young child is learning how to read both a book and a face, and the adolescent is learning chemical formulae as well as the formulae for successful friendships.

The educational curriculum

Children with Asperger's syndrome have an unusual profile of cognitive (i.e., thinking and learning) abilities. Teachers soon recognize that the child has a distinctive learning style, being talented in understanding the logical and physical world, noticing details and remembering and arranging facts in a systematic fashion (Baron-Cohen 2003). However, the child can be easily distracted when motivation is low. When solving academic problems the child appears to have a 'one-track mind' and a fear of failure. As the child progresses through the school grades, and especially during the high school years, teachers identify problems with organizational abilities, especially with regard to homework assignments and essays. They also observe that the child appears not to follow advice or learn from mistakes. End-of-year school reports often describe a conspicuously uneven profile of academic achievement, with areas of excellence alongside areas that require remedial assistance and increased attention and motivation.

In her section on learning and learning styles (see p. 55 onwards) Clare outlines the specific difficulties she and other people with Asperger's syndrome experienced due to having a different profile of cognitive abilities. The diagnosis of Asperger's syndrome itself gives limited information on a specific child's expected profile of cognitive abilities, but valuable information can be obtained from formal testing using a standardized test of intelligence and academic achievement. Standardized tests of intelligence have at least ten sub-tests that measure a range of intellectual abilities: some measure specific components of verbal reasoning, while others measure components of visual reasoning (Performance IQ). A person's Intelligence Quotient or IQ is usually divided into Verbal IQ, Performance IQ and an overall, or Full Scale, IQ.

Elizabeth Wurst, a colleague of Asperger, was the first to identify the variation in the profile of cognitive abilities associated with Asperger's syndrome. She and Asperger noted that many of the children they saw at the children's clinic in Vienna in the 1930s had a Verbal IQ significantly greater than their Performance IQ. A subsequent review of the cases seen by Asperger and his colleagues over three decades confirmed that 48 per cent of the children had a significantly higher Verbal IQ than Performance IQ (Hippler and Klicpera 2004). A similar discrepancy between Verbal IQ and Performance IQ for children with Asperger's syndrome has now been confirmed by several studies (Barnhill et al. 2000; Cederlund and Gillberg 2004; Dickerson Mayes and Calhoun 2003; Ehlers et al. 1997; Ghaziuddin and Mountain Kimchi 2004; Klin et al. 1995; Lincoln et al. 1988; Miller and Ozonoff 2000).

The roughly 50 per cent of children with Asperger's syndrome who have relatively advanced verbal reasoning skills may be colloquially described as 'verbalizers'. If such a child has difficulty acquiring a particular academic ability in the classroom, then his or her knowledge and understanding may be improved by reading about the concept or engaging in one-to-one discussion. About one in five children with Asperger's syndrome have relatively advanced visual reasoning skills and can be described as 'visualizers'. Here learning may be facilitated by observation, demonstration and visual imagery. The phrase 'a picture is worth a thousand words' is very applicable to such children.

Problems with attention and executive function

Research has confirmed that at least 75 per cent of children with Asperger's syndrome also have a profile of learning abilities indicative of an additional diagnosis of Attention Deficit Disorder (Fein et al. 2005; Goldstein and Schwebach, 2004; Holtmann, Bolte and Poustka 2005; Nyden et al. 1999; Schatz, Weimer and Trauner 2002; Sturm, Fernell and Gillberg 2004; Yoshida and Uchiyama 2004). Psychologists divide attention into four components: the ability to sustain attention, to pay attention to relevant information, to shift attention when needed, and to encode attention, that is, to remember what was attended to. Children with Asperger's syndrome appear to have problems with all four aspects of attention (Nyden et al. 1999). Remedial programs for children with Asperger's syndrome who have problems with attention will be very similar to those designed for children with Attention Deficit Disorder.

We now have considerable research evidence to confirm that some children, but more especially adolescents and adults with Asperger's syndrome, have impaired executive function (Goldberg et al. 2005; Goldstein, Johnson and Minshew 2001; Hughes, Russell and Robbins 1994; Joseph, McGrath and Tager-Flusberg 2005; Kleinhans, Akshoomoff and Delis 2005; Landa and Goldberg 2005; Ozonoff et al. 2004; Ozonoff, South and Provencal 2005; Prior and Hoffman 1990; Rumsey and Hamburger 1990; Shu et al. 2001; Szatmari et al. 1990). The psychological term *executive function* includes organizational and planning abilities, working memory, inhibition and impulse control, time management and prioritizing and understanding complex or abstract concepts. In the middle school years, problems with executive function can become apparent as the school curriculum changes to become more complex and self-directed, and teachers and parents have age appropriate expectations based on the maturing cognitive abilities of age peers. In the primary school years, success in subjects such as history can be measured by the ability to recall facts such as dates; by the middle school years, assessment in history has changed, and requires that the child shows ability in writing essays that have a clear organizational structure, and that he or she can recognize, compare and evaluate different perspectives and interpretations. Adolescents with impaired executive function have problems with the organizing and planning aspects of class work, assignments and homework. Teachers may complain that the adolescent with Asperger's syndrome can't seem to 'get his act together', and are critical of the child for being disorganized. Teachers need to recognize that this is a sign of impaired executive function and not necessarily due to the child's laziness or lack of commitment to school work.

Special interests

Although children with Asperger's syndrome have difficulties with the interpersonal and some of the cognitive aspects of life at school, most have remarkable ability in a chosen area of expertise. Clare describes special interests, or to use her term, 'obsessions', on p. 36. Unusual or special interests can develop as early as age two to three years (Bashe and Kirby 2001), and may commence with a preoccupation with parts of objects: spinning the wheels of toy cars, or manipulating electrical switches, for example. The next stage may be a fixation on something neither human nor toy (Pyles 2002), a fascination with a specific category of objects and the acquisition of as many examples as possible, or collecting fascinating facts on a specific topic such as the Titanic or volcanoes (Winter-Messiers 2007).

Much of the knowledge associated with the interest is self-directed and self-taught. The interest is chosen because of some aspect that is appealing or important to the child with Asperger's syndrome, not because the activity is the latest craze where a child wants to have the 'currency' of popularity. The interest is often a solitary and intuitive activity, pursued with great intensity, but often not shared with family members or peers. The degree of expertise and talent can be extraordinary and lead to success in school or national competitions for spelling or mathematics, for example, and the genuine admiration of others (Attwood 2003a).

The interest can be in the creative arts, such as an amazing ability in drawing or animation; attention to detail, photographic realism and use of colour can be outstanding. The art works are usually associated with the interest, for example oil paintings of steam trains. There may be rare qualities in music such as singing with perfect pitch, or an ability to communicate emotions in musical compositions and performances, which can appear to be in contrast to the difficulties the person has with the communication of emotions using speech and body language.

When a child with Asperger's syndrome has a special interest or a natural talent in a specific ability, it is important that teachers and parents develop such abilities to improve the child's self-esteem and status with other children, and remember that the interest could become a career. Adults with Asperger's syndrome are often employed for their expertise in a particular area.

Bullying, teasing and isolation

Clare has a chapter on the social environment in the playground and explains her experiences of being bullied, teased and isolated by other children (see page 76). I share and endorse her concerns regarding some of the potentially negative aspects of integration. Typical children are natural child psychologists and long before the child has a confirmed diagnosis, peers know that there is something different about the child. Parents and teachers hope that the integration will be enjoyable and successful, but while some peers will be welcoming, 'maternal' and kind to the child with Asperger's syndrome, others will be 'predatory' and consider the child as an easy target for teasing and bullying.

Children with Asperger's syndrome can be the victim of conventional acts of bullying and teasing, but they are particularly vulnerable to more subtle acts that can have devastating effects. Someone might openly steal a possession such as a hat and torment the child as he or she tries to retrieve it, engage in malicious gossip by spreading rumours, make comments that cause humiliation, or use obscene gestures and mocking. Another form of bullying that frequently occurs with children with Asperger's syndrome is peer shunning or social exclusion, such as not being included in a group at meal times, not having questions answered, deliberately being chosen last in a game or team, or not being invited to a social event. While parents and teachers encourage the child with Asperger's syndrome to interact with his or her peers, some children do not welcome the child's requests to join the conversation or activity. Improved social skills are of little practical value if peers deliberately and maliciously reject the child with Asperger's syndrome.

A recent study of the prevalence and frequency of bullying in a sample of more than 400 children with Asperger's syndrome reported a rate of bullying that was at least four times higher than for their peers (Little 2002). More than 90 per cent of mothers of children with Asperger's syndrome who completed the survey reported that their child had been the target of some form of bullying within the previous year. The pattern of bullying was different from that in the general population, with a higher-than-expected level of shunning and, in the teenage years, one in 10 adolescents with Asperger's syndrome was a victim of peer gang attack.

Research has confirmed that typical children who are the target of bullying are at greater risk for low self-esteem, increased levels of anxiety and depression, lower academic achievement, and increased social isolation (Hodges, Malone and Perry 1997; Ladd and Ladd 1998; Olweus 1992; Shtayermman 2007; Slee 1995). The psychological consequences of bullying for typical children can last for more than 10 years (Olweus 1992). Children with Asperger's syndrome are more prone to these consequences because of their already low self-esteem, predisposition to anxiety and difficulty understanding why someone would behave that way, as well as questioning why they were the target and what they could have done to avoid or stop it. Fortunately, we now have literature on how being bullied, teased and isolated affects children with Asperger's syndrome, and programs that can be implemented at school (see appendix on recommended resources).

Sensory and motor abilities

The social and cognitive abilities of children with Asperger's syndrome are easily recognised by teachers and parents, but we tend to pay less attention to their unusual sensory perception and movement abilities. This is despite the autobiographies of adults with Asperger's syndrome making frequent references to sensory experiences and to problems with coordination, ball skills and handwriting. Clare eloquently describes the sensory problems she and other children with Asperger's syndrome experience at school, especially in corridors and halls (see p. 99). Sport is an essential part of the school curriculum, and climbing and using adventure playground equipment are enjoyed by typical children. But those with Asperger's syndrome often experience tormenting and ridicule for not having the expected agility and dexterity of their peers, and they may actively avoid sports and playground equipment.

Sensory perception

Academics have only recently started to explore the sensory perception of children with Asperger's syndrome. Research studies and review papers have confirmed an unusual pattern of sensory perception and reaction (Dunn, Smith Myles and Orr 2002; Harrison and Hare 2004; Hippler and Klicpera 2004; Jones, Quigney and Huws 2003; Leekam et al. 2007; Minshew and Hobson 2008; O'Neil and Jones 1997; Rogers and Ozonoff 2005). Some adults with Asperger's syndrome consider their sensory sensitivity has a greater impact on their daily lives than problems with making friends, managing emotions and finding appropriate employment.

The most common sensitivity is to very specific sounds, but there can also be sensitivity to tactile experiences, light intensity, the taste and texture of food and specific aromas. There can be an under- or overreaction to the experience of pain and extreme temperatures, and the sense of balance, movement perception and body orientation can be unusual. One or several sensory systems can be affected so that everyday sensations in the classroom are perceived as unbearably intense or apparently not perceived at all. Teachers are often bewildered as to why these sensations are intolerable or not noticed, and the child with Asperger's syndrome is equally bewildered as to why other children and the teacher do not have the same level of sensitivity.

We have recently developed a conceptual and descriptive framework to examine the sensory experiences of children with Asperger's syndrome, and Bogdashina (2003) and Harrison and Hare (2004) have suggested that such children can have both hyper- and hyposensitivity to sensory experiences, sensory distortions, sensory 'tune outs' and sensory overload. It is important to identify which sensory experiences are perceived as painfully intense. The child may communicate distress to specific sounds such as the fire alarm or someone coughing by covering his or her ears, flinching or blinking in response to sudden noises. A sensory experience that is particularly aversive to children with Asperger's syndrome is shouting, which can occur on the playground and from a teacher in the classroom. There can be an aversion to and avoidance of specific aromas, such as the teacher's deodorant, or the tactile experiences of the school uniform or the reflected glare from the white board. Some of these experiences can be avoided, or the environment modified, or the child may be encouraged and commended for coping with aversive sensory experiences.

Movement and coordination

As much as children with Asperger's syndrome have a different way of thinking, they can also have a different way of moving (Attwood 2007). When walking or running, the child's coordination can be immature, with some children having a strange, sometimes idiosyncratic gait that lacks fluency and efficiency. Teachers often identify problems with fine motor skills, such as the ability to write and use scissors. Activities that require coordination and balance can also be affected, such as learning to ride a bicycle. Children with Asperger's syndrome can have difficulty knowing where their body is in space, which may often cause them to trip, bump into objects and spill drinks. The overall appearance can be of someone who is clumsy with the inevitable ridicule from peers and criticism from parents and teachers.

Movement skills can be assessed by observation and a range of standardized tests that measure specific movement abilities. For the naïve observer, there is an impression of clumsiness in the majority of children with Asperger's syndrome, but several studies using specialized assessment procedures have indicated that specific expressions of movement disturbance occur in almost all children with Asperger's syndrome (Ghaziuddin et al. 1994; Gillberg 1989; Gowen and Miall 2005; Green et al. 2002; Hippler and Klicpera 2004; Klin et al. 1995; Lopata et al. 2007; Manjiviona and Prior 1995; Miyahara et al. 1997).

The most common movement disturbance is Apraxia, that is, having problems with the conceptualization and planning of movement, so that the action is less proficient and coordinated than one would expect. Studies have indicated that children with Asperger's syndrome have problems with the mental preparation and planning of movement but have relatively intact motor pathways (Minshew, Goldstein and Siegel 1997; Rinehart et al. 2001; Rogers et al. 1996; Smith and Bryson 1998; Weimer et al. 2001). Thus poorly planned movement and a slow mental preparation time may be a more precise description than simply being clumsy.

Secondary mood disorders

Clare suggests that at least half of all people with Asperger's syndrome have a clinical depression at some point in their lives (see p. 53). Current research indicates that around 65 per cent of adolescents with Asperger's syndrome have an affective or mood disorder (Attwood 2003b). Perhaps the most common is an anxiety disorder (Ghaziuddin, Wieder-Mikhail and Ghaziuddin 1998; Gillot, Furniss and Walter 2001; Green et al. 2000; Kim et al. 2000; Konstantareas 2005; Russell and Sofronoff 2004; Tantam 2000; Tonge et al. 1999). However, the prevalence of depression is also high (Clarke et al. 1999; Gillot, Furniss and Walter 2001; Green et al. 2000; Kim et al. 2000; Konstantareas 2005). Research has indicated a greater risk of developing bipolar disorder (DeLong and Dwyer 1988; Frazier et al. 2002) and there is evidence to suggest an association with delusional disorders (Kurita 1999), paranoia (Blackshaw et al. 2001), and conduct disorders (Green et al. 2000; Tantam 2000). For teenagers with Asperger's syndrome, a secondary mood disorder is the rule rather than the exception.

Cognitive behaviour therapy

When a mood disorder is diagnosed in a child or adolescent with Asperger's syndrome, the clinical psychologist or psychiatrist will need to know how to modify psychological treatments for mood disorders to accommodate the unusual cognitive profile of children and adolescents with Asperger's syndrome. The primary psychological treatment for mood disorders is Cognitive Behaviour Therapy (CBT). We now have published case studies and research that indicate that CBT does significantly reduce mood disorders in children and adolescents with Asperger's syndrome (Bauminger 2002; Fitzpatrick 2004; Hare 1997; Reaven and Hepburn 2003; Sofronoff, Attwood and Hinton 2005; Sofronoff et al. 2007). Should the level of anxiety, depression or anger be of concern to parents and teachers, then it would be appropriate for the child or adolescent to be referred to the local child and adolescent mental health services.

Life after school

Over the last decade there has been an extraordinary increase in the number of children who have been diagnosed as having Asperger's syndrome. Those children are growing up and many are enrolling at college or university. In the past, some promising undergraduates with Asperger's syndrome have not been able to cope with the transition from school to university or college, with the need for greater independence skills (especially if the person leaves home) and the academic and social demands of being a student at university. The stress and lack of support can contribute to the development of an anxiety disorder or depression, and the possibility of withdrawal from the course. Fortunately, we now have greater knowledge of the support needed by university students with Asperger's syndrome (Fleisher 2003; Harpur, Lawlor and Fitzgerald 2004; Palmer 2006).

The college student with Asperger's syndrome will have to prepare for a very different lifestyle, and before enrolment there will need to be decisions made regarding accommodation, finances and practical and emotional support. There are advantages in students with Asperger's syndrome remaining at home, at least during the first college year, so that a parent can provide support with budgeting, issues of self-care (such as laundry, meal preparation and reminders regarding personal hygiene), and the organizational aspects required to complete course assignments on time, and also monitor the student's level of stress. If the student has to leave home, then the support services for undergraduates will need to know of the extra support and supervision that will probably be needed.

There is no career that would be impossible for a person with Asperger's syndrome. I have met several thousand adults with Asperger's syndrome who have had a very wide range of careers, from a part-time postman to the owner and chief executive of a successful international company. The list of professions includes engineering, accountancy, information technology, acting, teaching, psychology, and I have met musicians, artists, electricians, mechanics and wildlife rangers. Some people with Asperger's syndrome are able to achieve successful employment with very little support and encouragement, but for those who have difficulties finding the right job and maintaining employment, there are several books that provide advice for the individual, families, employment agencies and employers (Edmonds and Beardon 2008; Fast 2004; Grandin and Duffy 2004; Hawkins 2004; National Autistic Society 2005).

From my extensive clinical experience of people with Asperger's syndrome of all ages, and from knowing specific children and adults with Asperger's syndrome over several decades, I have observed that for some adults, the conspicuous signs of Asperger's syndrome can decrease over time. We recognize the continuum of expression of autism from the silent and aloof child to the person with Asperger's Syndrome. We have only just begun to explore the area of the autism continuum between Asperger's syndrome and the normal range. I have known some adolescents and adults with Asperger's syndrome who have progressed to a point on the continuum that only subtle differences and difficulties remain. The person has progressed to a description of personality rather than a diagnostic category used by psychologists and psychiatrists.

References

Attwood, T. (2000) 'Strategies for improving the social integration of children with Asperger syndrome.' *Autism 4*, 85–100.

Attwood, T. (2003a) 'Understanding and managing circumscribed interests.' In M. Prior (ed.) *Learning and Behavior Problems in Asperger Syndrome.* New York: The Guilford Press.

Attwood, T. (2003b) 'Frameworks for Behavioural Interventions.' *Child and Adolescent Psychiatric Clinics 12*, 65–86.

Attwood, T. (2007) *The Complete Guide to Asperger's Syndrome.* London: Jessica Kingsley Publishers.

Barnhill, G., Hagiwara, T., Smith Myles B. and Simpson R. (2000) 'Asperger Syndrome: A study of the cognitive profiles of 37 children and adolescents.' *Focus on Autism and Other Developmental Disabilities 15*, 146–160.

Baron-Cohen, S. (2003) *The Essential Difference: Men, Women and the Extreme Male Brain.* London: The Penguin Press.

Bashe, P. and Kirby, B.L. (2001) *The Oasis Guide to Asperger Syndrome.* New York: Crown Publishers.

Bauminger, N. (2002) 'The facilitation of social-emotional understanding and social interaction in high functioning children with autism: Intervention outcomes.' *Journal of Autism and Developmental Disorders 31*, 461–469.

Beaumont, R. and Sofronoff, K. (2008) 'A multi-component social skills intervention for children with Asperger syndrome: The junior Detective Training Program.' *Journal of Child Psychology and Psychiatry 49:7*, 743–753.

Blackshaw, A.J., Kinderman, P., Hare, D.J. and Hatton, C. (2001) 'Theory of mind, causal attribution and paranoia in Asperger syndrome.' *Autism 5*, 147–163.

Bogdashina, O. (2003) *Sensory Perceptual Issues in Autism and Asperger Syndrome: Different Sensory Experiences, Different Perceptual Worlds.* London: Jessica Kingsley Publishers.

Cederlund, M. and Gillberg, C. (2004) 'One hundred males with Asperger syndrome: a clinical study of background and associated factors.' *Developmental Medicine and Child Neurology 46*, 652–661.

Clarke, D., Baxter, M., Perry, D. and Prasher, V. (1999) 'Affective and psychotic disorders in adults with autism: seven case reports.' *Autism 3*, 149–164.

De Long G. and Dwyer J. (1988) 'Correlation of family history with specific autistic subgroups: Asperger's syndrome and bipolar affective disease.' *Journal of Autism and Developmental Disorders 18*, 593–600.

Dickerson Mayes, S. and Calhoun, S. (2003) 'Ability profiles in children with autism: influence of age and IQ.' *Autism 7*, 65–80.

Dubin, N. (2007) *Asperger Syndrome and Bullying.* London: Jessica Kingsley Publishers.

Dunn, W., Smith Myles, B. and Orr, S. (2002) 'Sensory processing issues associated with Asperger syndrome: a preliminary investigation.' *American Journal of Occupational Therapy 56*, 97–102.

Edmonds, G. and Beardon, L. (2008) *Asperger Syndrome & Employment*. London: Jessica Kingsley Publishers.

Ehlers, S. and Gillberg, C. (1993) 'The epidemiology of Asperger's Syndrome – A total population study.' *Journal of Child Psychology and Psychiatry 34*, 1327–1350.

Ehlers, S., Nyden, A., Gillberg, C., Dahlgren-Sandberg, A., Dahlgren, S.O., Hjelmquist, E. and Oden, A. (1997) 'Asperger syndrome, autism and attention disorders: a comparative study of the cognitive profiles of 120 children.' *Journal of Child Psychology and Psychiatry 38*, 207–217.

Eisenmajer, R., Prior, M., Leekham, S., Wing, L., Gould, J., Welham, M. and Ong, B. (1996) 'Comparison of clinical symptoms in autism and Asperger's disorder.' *Journal of the American Academy of Child and Adolescent Psychiatry 35*, 1523–1531.

Fast, Y. (2004) *Employment for Individuals with Asperger Syndrome or Non-Verbal Learning Disability: Stories and Strategies*. London: Jessica Kingsley Publishers.

Fein, D., Dixon, P., Paul, J. and Levin, H. (2005) 'Brief report: pervasive developmental disorder can evolve into ADHD: case illustrations.' *Journal of Autism and Developmental Disorders 35*, 525–534.

Fitzpatrick, E. (2004) 'The use of cognitive behavioural strategies in the management of anger in a child with an autistic disorder: an evaluation.' *Good Autism Practice 5*, 3–17.

Fleisher, M. (2003) *Making Sense of the Unfeasable: My Life Journey with Asperger syndrome*. London: Jessica Kingsley Publishers.

Frazier, J., Doyle, R., Chiu, S. and Coyle, J. (2002) 'Treating a child with Asperger's disorder and comorbid bipolar disorder.' *American Journal of Psychiatry 159*, 13–21.

Ghaziuddin, M. and Mountain Kimchi, K. (2004) 'Defining the intellectual profile of Asperger syndrome: comparison with High-Functioning Autism.' *Journal of Autism and Developmental Disorders 34*, 279–284.

Ghaziuddin, M., Butler, E., Tsai, L. and Ghaziuddin, N. (1994) 'Is clumsiness a marker for Asperger syndrome?' *Journal of Intellectual Disability Research 38*, 519–527.

Ghaziuddin, M., Wieder-Mikhail, W. and Ghaziuddin, N. (1998) 'Comorbidity of Asperger Syndrome: a preliminary report.' *Journal of Intellectual Disability Research 42*, 279–283.

Gillberg, C. (1989) 'Asperger's Syndrome in 23 Swedish children.' *Developmental Medicine and Child Neurology 31*, 520–31.

Gillot, A., Furniss, F. and Walter, A. (2001) 'Anxiety in high-functioning children with autism.' *Autism 5*, 277–286.

Goldberg, M., Mostofsky, S., Cutting, L., Mahone, E., Astor, B., Denckla, M. and Landa, R. (2005) 'Subtle executive impairment in children with autism and children with ADHD.' *Journal of Autism and Developmental Disorders 35*, 279–293.

Goldstein, G., Johnson, C. and Minshew, N. (2001) 'Attentional processes in autism.' *Journal of Autism and Developmental Disorders 31*, 433–440.

Goldstein, S. and Schwebach, A. (2004) 'The comorbidity of pervasive developmental disorder and attention deficit hyper-activity disorder: results of a retrospective chart review.' *Journal of Autism and Developmental Disorders 34*, 329–339.

Gowen, E. and Miall, C. (2005) 'Behavioural aspects of cerebella function in adults with Asperger syndrome.' *The Cerebellum 4*, 279–289.

Grandin, T. and Duffy, K. (2004) *Developing Talents: Careers for Individuals with Asperger Syndrome and High-Functioning Autism*. Kansas: Autism Asperger Publishing Company.

Green, D., Baird, G., Barnett, A., Henderson, L., Huber, J. and Henderson, S. (2002) 'The severity and nature of motor impairment in Asperger's syndrome: a comparison with specific developmental disorder of motor function.' *Journal of Child Psychology and Psychiatry 43*, 655–668.

Green, J., Gilchrist, A., Burton, D. and Cox, A. (2000) 'Social and psychiatric functioning in adolescents with Asperger Syndrome compared with conduct disorder.' *Journal of Autism and Developmental Disorders 30*, 279–293.

Hare, D.J. (1997) 'The use of Cognitive-Behavioural Therapy with people with Asperger Syndrome: a case study.' *Autism 1*, 215–225.

Harpur, J., Lawlor, M. and Fitzgerald, M. (2004) *Succeeding in College with Asperger Syndrome: A Student Guide*. London: Jessica Kingsley Publishers.

Harrison, J. and Hare, D. (2004) 'Brief report: Assessment of sensory abnormalities in people with autistic spectrum disorders.' *Journal of Autism and Developmental Disorders 34*, 727–730.

Hawkins, G. (2004) *How to Find Work that Works for People with Asperger Syndrome*. London: Jessica Kingsley Publishers.

Hippler, K. and Klicpera, C. (2004) 'A retrospective analysis of the clinical case records of "autistic psychopaths" diagnosed by Hans Asperger and his team at the University Children's Hospital, Vienna.' In U. Frith and E. Hill (eds) *Autism: Mind and Brain*. Oxford: Oxford University Press.

Hodges, E., Malone, J. and Perry, D. (1997) 'Individual risk and social risk as interacting determinants of victimization in the peer group.' *Developmental Psychology 32*, 1033–1039.

Holtmann, M., Bolte, S. and Poustka, F. (2005) 'Letters to the editor: ADHD, Asperger syndrome and High Functioning Autism. *Journal of the American Academy of Child and Adolescent Psychiatry 44*, 1101.

Howlin, P. and Asgharian, A. (1999) 'The diagnosis of autism and Asperger syndrome: findings from a survey of 770 families.' *Developmental Medicine and Child Neurology 41*, 834–839.

Hughes, C., Russell, J. and Robbins, T. (1994) 'Evidence for executive dysfunction in autism.' *Neuropsychologia 32*, 477–492.

Jones, R., Quigney, C. and Huws, J. (2003) 'First-hand accounts of sensory perceptual experiences in autism: a qualitative analysis.' *Journal of Intellectual and Developmental Disability 28*, 112–121.

Joseph, R., McGrath, L. and Tager-Flusberg, H. (2005) 'Executive dysfunction and its relation to language ability in verbal school-age children with autism.' *Developmental Neuropsychology 27*, 361–378.

Kadesjo, B., Gillberg, C. and Hagberg, B. (1999) 'Autism and Asperger syndrome in seven-year-old children: a total population study.' *Journal of Autism and Developmental Disorders 29*, 327–331.

Kim, J.A., Szatmari, P., Bryson, S.E., Streiner, D.L. and Wilson, F. (2000) 'The prevalence of anxiety and mood problems among children with autism and Asperger Syndrome.' *Autism 4*, 117–132.

Kleinhans, N., Akshoomoff, N. and Delis, D. (2005) 'Executive functions in autism and Asperger's disorder: flexibility, fluency and inhibition.' *Developmental Neuropsychology 27*, 379–401.

Klin, A., Volkmar, F., Sparrow, S., Cicchetti, D. and Rourke, B. (1995) 'Validity and neuropsychological characterization of Asperger Syndrome: convergence with Nonverbal Learning Disabilities Syndrome.' *Journal of Child Psychology and Psychiatry 36*, 1127–1140.

Konstantareas, M. (2005) 'Anxiety and depression in children and adolescents with Asperger syndrome.' In K. Stoddart (ed) *Children, Youth and Adults with Asperger Syndrome: Integrating Multiple Perspectives*. London: Jessica Kingsley Publishers.

Kurita, H. (1999) 'Brief report: delusional disorder in a male adolescent with high-functioning PDDNOS.' *Journal of Autism and Developmental Disorders 29*, 419–423.

Ladd, G. and Ladd, B.K. (1998) 'Parenting behaviours and parent-child relationships: correlates of peer victimization in kindergarden.' *Developmental Psychology 34*, 1450–1458.

Landa, R. and Goldberg, M. (2005) 'Language, social and executive functions in high-functioning autism: a continuum of performance.' *Journal of Autism and Developmental Disorders 35*, 557–573.

Leekam, S.R., Nieto, C., Libby, S.J., Wing, L. and Gould, J. (2007) 'Describing the Sensory Abnormalities of Children and Adults with Autism.' *Journal of Autism and Developmental Disorders 37*, 894–910.

Lincoln, A., Courchesne, E., Kilman, B., Elmasian, R. and Allen, M. (1988) 'A study of intellectual abilities in high-functioning people with autism.' *Journal of Autism and Developmental Disorders 18*, 505–524.

Little, L. (2002) 'Middle-class mothers' perceptions of peer and sibling victimization among children with Asperger syndrome and non-verbal learning disorders.' *Issues in Comprehensive Pediatric Nursing 25*, 43–57.

Lopata, C., Hamm, E.M., Volker, M.A., Sowinski, J.E. and Thomeer, M.L. (2007) 'Motor and visuomotor skills of children with Asperger's disorder: preliminary findings' *Perceptual and Motor Skills 104*, 1183–1192.

Manjiviona, J. and Prior, M. (1995) 'Comparison of Asperger's Syndrome and High-Functioning Autistic children on a test of motor impairment.' *Journal of Autism and Developmental Disorders 25*, 23–39.

Miller, J.N. and Ozonoff, S. (2000) 'The external validity of Asperger Disorder: lack of evidence from the domain of neuropsychology.' *Journal of Abnormal Psychology 109*, 227–238.

Minshew, N., Goldstein, G. and Siegel, D. (1997) 'Neuropsychologic functioning in autism: Profile of a complex information processing disorder.' *Journal of the International Neuropsychological Society 3*, 303–316.

Minshew, N.J. and Hobson, J.A. (2008) 'Sensory Sensitivities and Performance on Sensory Perceptual Tasks in High-functioning Individuals with Autism.' *(Journal of Autism and Developmental Disorders 38*, 1485–1498.

Miyahara, M., Tsujii, M., Hori, M., Nakanishi, K., Kageyama, H. and Sugiyama, T. (1997) 'Brief report: Motor incoordination in children with Asperger syndrome and learning disabilities.' *Journal of Autism and Developmental Disabilities 27*, 595–603.

National Autistic Society (2005) *Employing People with Asperger Syndrome: A Practical Guide.* London: The National Autistic Society.

Nyden, A., Gillberg, C., Hjelmquist, E. and Heiman, M. (1999) 'Executive function/attention deficits in boys with Asperger Syndrome, attention disorder and reading/writing disorder.' *Autism 3*, 213–228.

Olweus, D. (1992) 'Victimization by peers: antecedents and long-term outcomes.' In K.H. Rubin and J.B. Asenddorf (eds) *Social Withdrawal, Inhibition, and Shyness in Childhood.* Hillsdale, NJ: Lawrence Erlbaum Associates.

O'Neill, M. and Jones, R. (1997) 'Sensory-perceptual abnormalities in autism: a case for more research?' *Journal of Autism and Developmental Disorders 27*, 283–293.

Ozonoff, S., Cook, I., Coon, H., Dawson, G., Joseph, R., Klin, A., McMahon, W., Minshew, N., Munson, J., Pennington, B., Rogers, S., Spence, M., Tager-Flusberg, H., Volkmar, F. and Wrathall, D. (2004) 'Performance on Cambridge Neuropsychological Test Automated Battery Subtests sensitive to frontal lobe function in people with autistic disorder: evidence from the collaborative programs of excellence in autism network.' *Journal of Autism and Developmental Disorders 34*, 139–150.

Ozonoff, S., South, M. and Provencal, S. (2005) 'Executive functions.' In F. Volkmar, R. Paul, A. Klin and D. Cohen (eds) *Handbook of Autism and Pervasive Developmental Disorders, third edition.* New Jersey: John Wiley and Sons.

Palmer, A. (2006) *Realizing the College Dream with Autism or Asperger Syndrome: A Parent's Guide to Student Success.* London: Jessica Kingsley Publishers.

Prior, M. and Hoffmann, W. (1990) 'Neuropsychological testing of autistic children through an exploration with frontal lobe tests.' *Journal of Autism and Developmental Disorders 20*, 581–590.

Pyles, L. (2002) *Hitchhiking through Asperger Syndrome.* London: Jessica Kingsley Publishers.

Reaven, J. and Hepburn, S. (2003) 'Cognitive-behavioural treatment of obsessive-compulsive disorder in a child with Asperger syndrome.' *Autism 7*, 145–164.

Rinehart, N., Bradshaw, J., Brereton, A. and Tonge, B. (2001) 'Movement preparation in High-Functioning Autism and Asperger Disorder.' *Journal of Autism and Developmental Disorders 31*, 79–88.

Rogers, S., Benneto, L., McEvoy, R. and Pennington, B. (1996) 'Imitation and pantomime in high-functioning adolescents with autism spectrum disorders.' *Child Development 67*, 2060–2073.

Rogers, S. and Ozonoff, S. (2005) 'Annotation: What do we know about sensory dysfunction in autism? A critical review of the empirical evidence.' *Journal of Child Psychology and Psychiatry 46*, 1255–1268.

Rumsey, J. and Hamburger, S. (1990) 'Neuropsychological divergence of high-level autism and severe dyslexia.' *Journal of Autism and Developmental Disorders 20*, 155–168.

Russell, E. and Sofronoff, K. (2004) 'Anxiety and social worries in children with Asperger syndrome.' *Australian and New Zealand Journal of Psychiatry 39*, 633–638.

Schatz, A., Weimer, A. and Trauner (2002) 'Brief report: Attention differences in Asperger syndrome.' *Journal of Autism and Developmental Disorders 32*, 333–336.

Shtayermman, O. (2007) 'Peer victimization in adolescents and young adults diagnosed with Asperger's syndrome: A link to depressive symptomatology, anxiety symptomatology and suicidal ideation.' *Issues in Comprehensive Pediatric Nursing 30*, 87–107.

Shu, B., Lung, F., Tien, A. and Chen, B. (2001) 'Executive function deficits in non-retarded autistic children.' *Autism 5*, 165–174.

Slee, P. (1995) 'Peer victimization and its relationship to depression among Australian primary school students.' *Personal and Individual Differences 18*, 57–62.

Smith, I. and Bryson, S. (1998) 'Gesture imitation in autism: I. Nonsymbolic postures and sequences.' *Cognitive Neuropsychology 15*, 747–770.

Sofronoff, K., Attwood, T. and Hinton, S. (2005) 'A randomised controlled trial of a CBT intervention for anxiety in children with Asperger syndrome.' *Journal of Child Psychology and Psychiatry 46*, 1152–1160.

Sofronoff, K., Attwood, T., Hinton, S. and Levin, I. (2007) 'A randomized controlled trial of a Cognitive Behavioural Intervention for anger management in children diagnosed with Asperger syndrome.' *Journal of Autism and Developmental Disorders 37*, 1203–1214.

Sturm, H., Fernell, E. and Gillberg, C. (2004) 'Autism spectrum disorders in children with normal intellectual levels: associated impairments and subgroups.' *Developmental Medicine and Child Neurology 46*, 444–447.

Szatmari, P., Tuff, L., Finlayson, A. and Bartolucci, G. (1990) 'Asperger's syndrome and autism: neurocognitive aspects.' *Journal of the American Academy of Child and Adolescent Psychiatry 29*, 130–136.

Tantam, D. (2000) 'Psychological disorder in adolescents and adults with Asperger disorder.' *Autism 4*, 47–62.

Tonge, B., Brereton, A., Gray, K. and Einfeld, S. (1999) 'Behavioural and emotional disturbance in high-functioning autism and Asperger Syndrome.' *Autism 3*, 117–130.

Weimer, A., Schatz, A., Lincoln, A., Ballantyne, A. and Trauer, D. (2001) "Motor" impairment in Asperger syndrome: evidence for a deficit in proprioception.' *Developmental and Behavioral Pediatrics 22*, 92–101.

Willey, L.H. (1999) *Pretending to be Normal: Living with Asperger's Syndrome.* London: Jessica Kingsley Publishers.

Wing, L. (1981) 'Asperger's Syndrome: A clinical account.' *Psychological Medicine 11*, 115–130.

Winter-Messiers, M.A. (2007) 'From Tarantulas to Toilet Brushes: Understanding the Special Interest Areas of Children and Youth With Asperger Syndrome.' *Remedial and Special Education, 28(3)*, 140–152.

Yoshida, Y. and Uchiyama, T. (2004) 'The clinical necessity for assessing Attention Deficit/Hyperactivity Disorder (AD/HD) symptoms in children with high functioning Pervasive Developmental Disorders (PDD).' *European Journal of Child and Adolescent Psychiatry 13*, 307–314.

Recommended Resources: Books to help with friendship skills

Friendship from 3–6 years

Berry, J. (1996) *Let's Talk About: Being Helpful.* New York: Scholastic Inc.

Rogers, F. (1987) *Mr Roger's Neighbourhood: Making Friends.* New York: The Putnam and Grosset Group.

The *Mr. Men* books, by Roger Hargreaves, can encourage the development of characterization skills and are published in America by Price Stern Sloan and in the United Kingdom and Australia by Ladybird and Penguin Books.

Friendship from 6–9 years

Brandenberg, A. (1995) *Communication: is telling and listening.* London: Mammoth.

Brown, L.K. and Brown, M. (1998) *How to Be a Friend: A Guide to Making Friends and Keeping Them.* Boston: Little, Brown and Company.

Buehner, C. (1998) *I Did It, I'm Sorry.* New York: Puffin Books.

Howley, M. and Arnold, E. (2005) *Revealing the Hidden Social Code.* London: Jessica Kingsley Publishers.

Howlin, P., Baron-Cohen, S. and Hadwin, J. (1999) *Teaching Children with Autism to Mind-Read.* Chichester: John Wiley and Sons.

Leedy, L. (1996) *How Humans Make Friends.* New York: Holiday House.

McGrath, H. (1997) *Dirty Tricks: Classroom games for teaching social skills.* Melbourne: Adison Wesley Longman.

McGrath, H. and Francey, S. (1991) *Friendly Kids Friendly Classrooms: teaching social skills and confidence in the classroom.* Melbourne: Adison Wesley Longman.

Roffey, S., Tarrant, T. and Majors, K. (1994) *Young Friends: Schools and Friendship*. London: Cassell Publishers.

Schroeder, A. (1997) *The Socially Speaking Game*. Wisbech, Cambs: LDA: a division of McGraw-Hill children's publishing. More information at www.LDAlearning.com

Wilson, C. (1993) *Room 14: A social language program*. East Moline, IL: Linguisystems.

Friendship from 9–13 years

American Girl Library (1996) *The Care and Keeping of Friends*. Middleton, WI: Pleasant Company Publications.

Crooke, P.J., Hendrix, R.E. and Rachman, J.Y. (2008) 'Brief Report: Measuring the Effectiveness of Teaching Social Thinking to Children with Asperger Syndrome (AS) and High Functioning Autism (HFA).' *Journal of Autism and Developmental Disorders 38*, 581–591.

Schmidt, J. (1997) *Making and Keeping Friends: Ready-to-use lessons, stories and activities for building relationships (grades 4–8)*. Greenville, NC: Brookcliff Publishers.

Judge Judy Sheindlin (2001) *You Can't Judge a Book by it's Cover: Cool Rules for School*. New York: Cliff Street Books: an imprint of HarperCollins Publishers.

Judge Judy Sheindlin (2001) *Win or Lose by How you Choose*. New York: Cliff Street Books: an imprint of HarperCollins Publishers.

Lawrence, C. (2008) *How to Make School Make Sense*. London: Jessica Kingsley Publishers.

Friendship in adolescence

Beck, T.A. (1994) *Building Healthy Friendships: Teaching Friendship Skills to Young People*. Saratoga, CA: R and E Publishers.

Canfield, J., Hanson, M.V. and Kirberger, K. (1998) *Chicken Soup: Teenage Soul Journal*. Deerfield Beach, FL: Health Communications Inc.

Cornelius, H. and Faire, S. (1998) *Everyone Can Win: How to Resolve Conflict*. Roseville, NSW, Australia: Simon and Schuster.

Decker, B. (1996) *The Art of Communicating: Achieving Interpersonal Impact in Business*, revised edition. Menlo Park, CA: Crisp Publications Inc.

Gabor, D. (2001) *How to Start a Conversation and Make Friends*. Revised and Updated. New York: Simon and Schuster Publishers.

Harpur, J., Lawlor, M. and Fitzgerald, M. (2006) *Succeeding with Interventions for Asperger Syndrome Adolescents*. London: Jessica Kingsley Publishers.

Lawson, W. (2006) *Friendships. The Aspie Way*. London: Jessica Kingsley Publishers.

Matthews, A. (1990) *Making Friends: A Guide to Getting Along with People*. Singapore: Media Masters.

McGrath, H. and Edwards, H. (1997) *Friends: A practical guide to understanding relationships*. Marrickville, NSW, Australia: CHOICE Books.

Pease, A. (1995) *Body Language: How to read others' thought by their gestures.* Mona Vale, NSW, Australia: Camel Publishing Company.

Bullying and teasing of children with Asperger's syndrome

Attwood, T. (2004) 'Strategies to reduce the bullying of young children with Asperger Syndrome.' *Australian Journal of Early Childhood 29,* 15–23.

Dubin, N. (2007) *Asperger Syndrome and Bullying.* London: Jessica Kingsley Publishers.

Gray, C. and Williams, J. (2006) *No Fishing Allowed: Reel in" Bullying.* Arlington, TX: Future Horizons.

Heinrichs, R. (2003) *Perfect Targets: Asperger Syndrome and Bullying: Practical Solutions for Surviving the Social World.* Kansas: Autism Asperger Publishing Company.

The social curriculum

Social skills programs designed for children and adults with Asperger's syndrome:

Beaumont, R. and Sofronoff, K. (2008) 'A multi-component social skills intervention for children with Asperger syndrome: The junior Detective Training Program.' *Journal of Child Psychology and Psychiatry 49:7,* 743–753.

Bereket, R. (2005) *Playing it Right: Social Skills activities for parents and teachers of young children with Aspergers, autism and PDD: Age 3+.*

Carter, M. and Santomauro, J. (2004) *Space Travellers: An interactive program for developing social understanding, social competence and social skills for students with Asperger Syndrome, Autism and other social cognitive challenges.* Kansas: Autism Asperger Publishing Company.
More information at www.asperger.net

Garcia Winner, M. (2000) *Inside Out: What makes a person with social cognitive deficits tick?* San Jose, CA: Michelle Garcia Winner.
More information at www.socialthinking.com

Garcia Winner, M. (2002) *Thinking about YOU Thinking about ME: Philosophy and strategies to further develop perspective taking and communication abilities for persons with Social Cognitive Deficits.* San Jose, CA: Michelle Garcia Winner.
More information available at www.socialthinking.com

Gutstein, S. and Steely, R. (2002a) *Relationship Development Intervention with Young Children: Social and emotional development activities for Asperger syndrome, autism, PDD and NLD.* London: Jessica Kingsley Publishers.

Gutstein, S. and Steely, R. (2002b) *Relationship Development Intervention with Older Children, Adolescents and Adults: Social and emotional development activities for Asperger syndrome, autism, PDD and NLD.* London: Jessica Kingsley Publishers.

McAfee, J. (2002) *Navigating the Social World: A curriculum for individuals with Asperger's syndrome, High Functioning Autism and Related Disorders.* Arlington, TX: Future Horizons.
More information at www.futurehorizons-autism.com

Moyes, R.A. (2001) *Incorporating Social Goals in the Classroom.* London: Jessica Kingsley Publishers.

Introduction to
Martian in the Playground

If you are wondering what a child with Asperger's syndrome is thinking, feeling and experiencing at school, *Martian in the Playground* will let you know. It is an excellent book and my copy has highlighted text on almost every page. It is essential reading for teachers, but I suspect that it will also provide valuable insight for parents and adults with Asperger's syndrome.

The descriptions are not solely from Clare's perspective, as she includes quotations from 25 adults with Asperger's syndrome and incorporates the theoretical models of Autism Spectrum Disorders in her explanations. These sometimes uninspiring theories become fascinating when Clare describes how they affect the school life of someone with Asperger's syndrome. She starts with an explanation of the diagnostic issues and terms and emphasises both the abilities and the disabilities. One of the confusing aspects of Asperger's syndrome for teachers is the discrepancy between the child's areas of impairment and excellence. I often note that school reports refer to high grades in some subjects and failure in others; this is due to the unusual intellectual profile associated with Asperger's syndrome. The research on IQ profiles indicates that children with Asperger's syndrome have good factual and lexical (word) knowledge. Their highest scores are often on the subtests that measure vocabulary, general knowledge and verbal problem solving. Such children have an impressive vocabulary and their recall of facts can make them popular in a Trivial Pursuit team. Their lowest performance tends to be on tests that require the mental manipulation of information (i.e., 'multi tracking'), or in tasks in which the child is easily distracted, or those which are affected by the child being a ponderous perfectionist.

Clare rightly states that there can be different assumptions about the purpose of attending school, and often the child's perspective regarding the value of school is unknown or ignored. Typical children enjoy the social aspects of school – making and meeting friends – and especially look forward to the breaks to socialize. Children with Asperger's syndrome have considerable difficulty with the social aspects of school, particularly making friends, and are often aware of being different to their peers and more vulnerable to being ridiculed, tormented and rejected. Socializing is usually an exhausting intellectual rather than intuitive activity. The conventional purpose of attending school is to acquire academic knowledge, but the learning environment of a typical classroom is not designed for the cognitive, sensory and emotional profile of children with Asperger's syndrome. It is not surprising that some children with Asperger's syndrome are so reluctant to attend school. Clare's book will highlight many of the issues, and provide teachers with an understanding of the challenges faced every day by a child with Asperger's syndrome, so that school can become an Asperger Friendly environment.

Clare has very strong opinions regarding labelling, normalization and inclusion which I endorse. When I ask adults who have acquired a diagnosis in their later years when they would have preferred to know about their diagnosis, the invariable response is 'as early as possible'. This would have prevented so many of the problems associated with low self-esteem and being frequently misunderstood, in terms of both their abilities and intentions. It would also have facilitated better decisions regarding employment and relationships. It would have encouraged changes in the presentation of the curriculum and methods of assessment, and school would have been a much happier experience for the child and his or her teachers.

Children with Asperger's syndrome have often discovered strategies to accommodate their idiosyncratic learning style. For some, talking to themselves during an activity can be a way of vocalizing thinking to improve problem solving. While this strategy is beneficial for the child, it can be distracting to other children and annoy the teacher. Unless an alternative and equally effective strategy can be suggested, it would be wise to focus on the volume of the self-talk rather than discouraging it all together. My approach to what appears to be eccentric behaviour is to first establish the function of the behaviour from the child's perspective and then achieve a compromise or acquire a mutually acceptable alternative.

Children with Asperger's syndrome are affected more than typical children by sensory experiences, have a limited ability to cope with change, and have unusual cognitive and language abilities and motor coordination problems. They can be extremely sensitive to specific sounds such as the sharp noise of a chair scraping on the floor or the squeak of pens on a marker board. Bright sunlight shining on the page or white board can cause a disturbance of visual processing, and the aromas of classroom equipment such as art materials or cleaning products can be perceived as extremely nauseous. Clare provides quotations to explain the sensory experiences of children with Asperger's syndrome. A teacher needs to be aware of how sensory perception can affect learning and behaviour.

Change can be very stressful for children with Asperger's syndrome. We all have a variable capacity to cope with the unexpected but such children have a very limited capacity to cope with change. They prefer routines and certainty. While spontaneity and unpredictability can be enjoyable aspects of the curriculum or personality of the teacher for most children, they can create considerable anxiety for a child with Asperger's syndrome. Clare describes the value of a structured classroom in terms of the clearly visible and known order of activities and events.

She also describes a characteristic that has not been recognised in previous literature for teachers, namely, distraction from within. We know that such children have many of the characteristics associated with attention deficit disorder. In particular they may have problems maintaining and switching attention. They can also be distracted by inner thoughts or daydreams. Typical children can be prone to daydreaming, but children with Asperger's syndrome can replay in their mind a whole television programme or film, so that the 'daydream' lasts the duration of the original film, without a mental 'pause' button to get back to the work in hand.

The characteristics of attention deficit disorder can include problems with organizational and planning abilities. Clare states that teachers need to recognize that a delay in completing assignments is not simply due to laziness. There can be genuine problems with time perception and management, the child simply not knowing how long it will take to complete a project. She also explains why children with Asperger's syndrome often describe specific activities as boring, or refuse to comply with requests that, from the child's perspective, are illogical. I have found that a child's compliance and motivation can be encouraged by logic rather than punishment.

Children with Asperger's syndrome also have an unusual profile of linguistic abilities, including a tendency to make a literal interpretation of what is said (teachers who use sarcasm, please note). Such children can also have difficulty focusing on the teacher's voice when there is background chatter from nearby children. They may not have been able to distinguish the instruction from the confusing jumble of sounds from their peers. When they ask for help or for the information to be repeated, it may be because of problems with auditory processing rather than inattentiveness.

Children with Asperger's syndrome have a different way of thinking, learning and perceiving, and also a different way of moving. Although they may be described as clumsy, research suggests that a more precise description is a problem with mental preparation time for the movement. This will obviously effect coordination, especially in sports and physical education classes. There is also a likelihood of problems with handwriting. My opinion is that handwriting is an obsolete skill. How may handwritten letters do you receive? It would be wise to teach typing rather than handwriting.

School is more than just the classroom, and the child who has Asperger's syndrome can feel that he or she is an alien in the playground. Clare's title is an accurate description of the playground experiences of such children. The playground can be frightening, due to the noise level (especially the shrieking and shouting), so many children intent on socializing or teasing, and the lack of structure and purpose. Children with Asperger's syndrome need times in their school day to be alone, relax in solitude, think without interruption and feel safe. But at school, how can you be alone? If you do want to socialize, who would want to be your friend if you have Asperger's syndrome? And if you find someone who could be a friend, how do you make and keep that friend? These aspects of school life are often not acknowledged by teachers as more important to the child with Asperger's syndrome than academic success. Guidance in friendship skills may not be assumed as a teacher's responsibility or the attitude may be, 'Well, if he hasn't any friends, he should just try harder'. Clare outlines the aspects of the social environment in the playground and classroom that affect social integration, acceptance and friendship.

A lack of success academically and socially at school can lead to low self-esteem and depression, anxiety and fear of failure (academically and socially). It can also result in anger at individuals or school representatives for the feeling of alienation. Clare explains the psychological aspects of being a *Martian in the playground* and teachers will benefit from understanding the psychological world of the child with Asperger's syndrome. If you are a teacher, you need to read this book, and when you have, use the insight and wisdom you have acquired to improve the abilities and quality of life for a child with Asperger's syndrome.

I
Introduction

Clare continues to be rather a loner and becomes noticeably upset if other children try to include her in their games or activities ... She is not very helpful in the classroom and can be very obstinate ... She finds it hard to follow general instructions and quickly panics. She is very self-centred ... inclined to daydream ... has difficulty working with others ... often sullen and determined not to co-operate. She dislikes being given a direct order ... Clare's difficulty to get on with people is impeding her learning as she cuts herself off and does not listen attentively ... tantrums ... After a determined start at the beginning of the term to play with the other children, she has now relapsed and is more alone than ever.

(extracts from my primary school reports)

Here is one of my most vivid memories of school: I am standing in a corner of the playground as usual, as far away as possible from people who might bump into me or shout, gazing into the sky and absorbed in my own thoughts. I am eight or nine years old and have begun to realize that I am different in some nameless but all-pervasive way.

I don't understand the children around me. They frighten and confuse me. They don't want to talk about things that are interesting. I used to think that they were silly, but now I am beginning to understand that I am the one who is all wrong. I try so hard to do what I am told, but just when I think I am being most helpful and good, the teachers tell me off and I don't know why. It's as if everybody is playing some complicated game and I am the only one who hasn't been told the rules. But no-one will admit that it's a game or that there are rules, let alone explain them to me. Maybe it's all a joke being played on me; I know about "jokes". I would be happy if they left me alone to think my thoughts, but they won't.

I think that I might be an alien who has been put on this planet by mistake; I hope that this is so, because this means that there might be other people out there in the universe like me. I dream that one day a spaceship will fall from the sky onto the tarmac in front of me, and the people who step out of the spaceship will tell me, "It's all been a dreadful mistake. You were never meant to be here. We are your people and now we've come to take you home."

In the next few years, I would work out that the spaceship was never going to come and rescue me, but it wasn't until I was twenty that I finally found a name for my differences, when I was diagnosed with Asperger's syndrome, a mild form of autism. Five years later, looking back at my schooldays, I feel regret and anger for the needless pain I went through and for the energy that I and my teachers wasted pointlessly. If the right people had only been given the right information, more than a decade of my life might have gone very differently. Talking to other adults with Asperger's syndrome, I found that the same regret and anger were almost universal (in fact, my school experiences were far better than those of many others: I was academically able in many areas, had several good and sympathetic teachers, and the teasing and bullying that I experienced was comparatively mild).

It would be nice to think that things had changed since my school days, but, in discussions, teenagers still at school today described the same problems and issues as people in their thirties and forties (many of these school problems, incidentally, were described in Hans Asperger's original paper in 1944). In the '80s and '90s, awareness of and research into Asperger's syndrome increased dramatically, but it is still taking considerable time for this new knowledge to reach teachers and others "on the ground".

Consequently, people with Asperger's syndrome are often passionate about sharing our knowledge of and insights into Asperger's syndrome, in the hope that the next generation of children with Asperger's may not have to go through what we did. We don't need ramps or expensive equipment to make a difference for us; all we need is understanding. As one young man with Asperger's, Simon, commented, "I think the main problem with AS is simply a lack of awareness."

In recent years, several excellent guides to Asperger's syndrome by professionals have been published, including a couple aimed specifically at teachers (I've included a list of some of the best of these in the appendices). It would be redundant to duplicate this material, and in any case, I am neither a researcher (although I read as widely as I can in the research literature on Asperger's syndrome and autism), nor a teacher (although I work part-time at a school for children with autism and Asperger's syndrome, the particular children I work with are severely disabled, sometimes non-verbal, and so face very different educational challenges). My only qualifications for writing this book are that I have Asperger's syndrome and was once a schoolchild.

However, many teachers and other professionals who work with children and young people with Asperger's have said to me that, while the practical advice and information provided by books written by professionals are indispensable, they still find it very hard to understand "what goes on in the head" of many of their students – what's it's actually like to be a schoolchild with Asperger's syndrome. They report that autobiographical accounts by people with Asperger's and other forms of autism have been uniquely helpful, and have enabled them to empathise with their students to a much greater degree, but obviously any autobiography can only describe the experiences of one individual, who may be more or less typical, and will cover many aspects of life other than school.

This book is not intended to replace but to complement those written by professionals and by other people with Asperger's. I can't advise on what teaching strategies are most effective with students with Asperger's syndrome or provide practical tips. I can only describe what I and others experienced as children. I will try to communicate something of the subjective experience of school for children with Asperger's syndrome, in the hope that this will equip teachers to approach such students with greater understanding. In keeping with this goal, I have generally avoided quoting from texts by professionals in favour of first-person quotes from people with Asperger's syndrome. I have occasionally quoted from professionals either to back up the personal impressions of people with Asperger's with research or when a comment has seemed particularly insightful. However, I have read extensively among accounts by professionals, parents and teachers in attempting to understand how they perceive us and why they sometimes react to us in the ways that they do.

In the following chapter, I have given a brief "beginner's guide to Asperger's syndrome", summarizing basic information on the features of the syndrome, before going on to examine what this means "from the inside", first in terms of overall perceptions of education and its goals, and then in practical terms, examining the experiences of schoolchildren with Asperger's not only in the classroom but also in areas of school which are often ignored or not considered to be of educational interest, but which often loomed as large in people's memories as anything that happened in the classroom. Inevitably, the division into chapters is somewhat arbitrary – many problems spill over from the classroom to the corridors or vice versa. I have devoted separate chapters to the topics of "challenging behaviour", preparing for the world outside school, and finally to one issue rarely addressed by professional textbooks but of crucial importance to people with Asperger's syndrome: sharing knowledge about Asperger's syndrome with the pupil themselves.

In writing this book, I have drawn not only on my own memories but also on the accounts, experiences, and opinions volunteered by many other people with Asperger's (including people from the UK, the USA, New Zealand, Sweden, Canada and the Netherlands), who generously granted their permission for me to quote them and encouraged me to pursue this project. I hope that I have managed to convey something of the diversity of people with Asperger's syndrome, as well as the things we have in common.

For far too many people with Asperger's, as Jack commented, " ... *all* of school was either terrifying or totally boring ...". Hopefully this book may do a little to change things.

A note on terminology

Like many other people with autistic spectrum conditions (see Sinclair 1999), I object to the insistence on using "people-first" language by referring to "people with autism" instead of "autistic people". We are not people who "just happen to have" autism; it is not an appendage that can be separated from who we are as people, nor is it something shameful that has to be reduced to a subclause. As Sinclair notes, "It is only when someone has decided that the characteristic being referred to is negative that suddenly people want to separate it from the person."

A note on quotations

All quotations for which I have not cited a published source are from people with Asperger's syndrome. Some of the names given are real names, while others are pseudonyms; I have respected individual preferences about this wherever possible.

2
What is Asperger's Syndrome?

For all of my life, I was the 'different' kid …

(Fred)

Asperger's syndrome (AS) is generally considered to be a mild form of autism, a developmental disorder of neurological origin which affects very approximately at least one in every thousand people (estimates vary wildly, depending on how broad the definition used is, and its actual prevalence is made even harder to estimate since, until very recently, many or most people with Asperger's went undiagnosed) and which affects communication and social interaction.

On the basis of current research, it appears that autism can have many different causes, such as prenatal rubella or Fragile-X syndrome, but that there is a significant genetic factor involved in many cases (it has been noted by many researchers, from Hans Asperger on, that some parents or relatives of children with Asperger's syndrome will display traits of the syndrome themselves). Although autism was once believed by some to be a form of emotional disturbance resulting from bad parenting, this theory has been completely discredited, and for the last three decades, all serious researchers have agreed that autism is wholly biological in nature.

Asperger's Syndrome
High Functioning Autism
Pervasive Development Disorder/not otherwise specified
Semantic-Pragmatic Disorder…
Abbreviations: AS; HFA; PDD – NOS; SPD

Many autistic people also have some degree of learning difficulties (formerly known as "mental handicap"), but autism can also co-exist with average or higher-than-average intelligence. Autistic people who have relatively good intellectual and verbal abilities are often referred to as having "high-functioning autism" (HFA). Recently, many researchers have suggested that it is most accurate to see the category of autism as a continuum – the "autistic spectrum" – ranging from the most severely disabled people, who may never develop speech, to the most high-functioning.

The group of children first described by Hans Asperger in 1944 generally displayed much better language and communication skills than those described in the same year by Leo Kanner, the discoverer of autism. Asperger's paper was largely neglected until the late 70s and early 80s, when the label "Asperger's syndrome" was revived by researchers such as Lorna Wing (1981) as a way of describing more able and verbal autistic spectrum children. The relationship between Asperger's syndrome and high-functioning autism is still subject to debate (see Schopler 1998 for an exhaustive review), although it is agreed that Asperger's syndrome is clearly part of the autistic spectrum. Many researchers believe that there is no meaningful distinction between the two groups.

Currently, the official diagnostic criteria most often used, those of DSM-IV (the fourth edition of the American Psychiatric Association's *Diagnostic and Statistical Manual of Mental Disorders 1994*) distinguish Asperger's syndrome from autism on the basis of the absence of general delay in language and cognitive skills.

However, it is unclear whether this distinction really identifies two separate conditions, or whether it would be more useful to speak of autism with and without language delay or learning difficulties. At present, people of average or above average IQ with an autistic spectrum condition tend to receive the label of "high-functioning autism" if they have had a history of language delay as children, and "Asperger's syndrome" if not (even though they may, like me, have had language development which, while not delayed, was extremely odd). Many children show some language delay in early childhood while going on to fit Asperger's description with great exactness. As Peeters and Gillberg (1999, p.30) argue, "it is so rare for an individual on the autistic spectrum to have perfectly normal language development, that the inclusion of 'normal language development' as a criterion for diagnosis does not make clinical sense". They point out that on these grounds, many of Asperger's original cases would not have met current diagnostic criteria for Asperger's syndrome. Once initial language delay has been overcome, it does not seem possible to find further distinctions between the two groups. This is not to imply homogeneity: people at the mild/high-functioning end of the autistic spectrum are an extremely diverse bunch and the study of various subgroups may well be a productive area for future research. Some of the people I have quoted define themselves as having "high-functioning autism" as distinct from "Asperger's syndrome". But the many differences between us do not seem to be adequately pinned down by a simple distinction between those with and those without histories of language delay.

DSM-IV:
299.80 Asperger's Disorder

(A) *Qualitative impairment in social interaction, as manifested by at least two of the following:*

1. marked impairment in the use of multiple nonverbal behaviors such as eye-to-eye gaze, facial expression, body postures and gestures to regulate socialinteraction
2. failure to develop peer relationships appropriate to developmental level
3. a lack of spontaneous seeking to share enjoyment, interests, or achievements with other people (e.g., by a lack of showing, bringing, or pointing out objectsof interest to other people)
4. lack of social or emotional reciprocity.

(B) *Restricted repetitive and stereotyped patterns of behavior, interests and activities as manifested by at least one of the following:*

1. encompassing preoccupation with one or more stereotyped and restricted patterns of interest that is abnormal either in intensity or focus
2. apparently inflexible adherence to specific, non-functional routines or rituals
3. stereotyped and repetitive motor mannerisms (e.g., hand or finger flapping or twisting or complex whole-body movements)
4. persistent preoccupation with parts of objects.

(C) *The disturbance causes clinically significant impairment in social, occupa-tional or other important areas of functioning.*

(D) *There is no clinically significant general delay in language (e.g., singlewords used by age 2 years, communicative phrases used by age 3 years).*

(E) *There is no clinically significant delay in cognitive development or in the development of age-appropriate self-help skills, adaptive behavior (other than in social interaction) and curiosity about the environment in childhood.*

(F) *Criteria are not met for another specific Pervasive Developmental Disorder or Schizophrenia.*

"Pervasive developmental disorder not otherwise specified" (PDD-NOS) is a term sometimes used (particularly in the United States) for people who seem to be on the autistic spectrum, but who do not, in the opinion of the clinician, meet all the diagnostic criteria for a formal diagnosis of autism or AS (before the diagnosis of PDD-NOS was introduced, many of these people were given even vaguer diagnoses such as "autistic tendencies" or "autistic-like"). Many people feel that PDD is an unhelpful diagnosis and that "autistic spectrum disorder" might be more useful.

> I was born and diagnosed at around 3 with around half the symptoms of autism. My Montessori school teacher noticed that I wasn't making eye contact with the rest of the children and that I didn't play with them, just isolated myself 'in my own little world'. At first the professionals thought that I might have 'full-blown' autism, however at one of my evaluations I was a wee bit too social to fit that diagnostic category. So ... what do professionals do when they want to say 'I don't know exactly what's going on here?' but don't want to sacrifice their professional pride? They make up a fancy name like 'development deviations' or 'neurological developmental disorder – mixed, diagnosis deferred' or more recently, PDD-NOS, 'pervasive developmental disorder – not otherwise specified' ... not fitting anyone's categories or expectations is the story of my life.
> (Karen)

"Semantic-pragmatic disorder" (SPD) is another much debated term, with many autism researchers suggesting that it is simply a label for mild autistic spectrum conditions as viewed by speech and language therapists (see Bishop 1989). Within the UK's National Autistic Society, professionals no longer use "semantic-pragmatic disorder" as a separate diagnosis (Shields, not dated). As many professionals and researchers have pointed out, exactly which diagnosis a child receives (high-functioning autism, Asperger's syndrome, PDD-NOS, or semantic-pragmatic disorder) seems to be dependent more on where they live and which professionals they are seen by first, than on the details of their condition itself.

For the sake of clarity, I will use "Asperger's syndrome" throughout this book to refer to all children and adults who (whatever their past language development) presently fit the pattern described by Hans Asperger in his original paper, whether their official diagnosis (if they have one at all) is of Asperger's syndrome, high-functioning autism, or PDD-NOS (similarly, I will use "schoolchildren" to encompass all ages between 4 and 18). The exact diagnosis received seems to make remarkably little difference to school experiences once language has developed and the people I have quoted from range from those who developed language unusually early to some who did not develop communicative speech until as late as 6 (or in one case, 7) years old.

Almost all of the 25 different people from whom I have quoted (26 counting myself), and the many other people with whom I discussed the issues described in the book, have a formal diagnosis of Asperger's, autism or PDD-NOS; however, because of the shortage of facilities for diagnosing adults in many areas, some are still in the process of seeking an official label. Nonetheless, the issues they faced as schoolchildren are the same (I made no attempt at random sampling, and we may well be atypical in being able to describe our experiences with unusual articulacy).

The "Triad of Impairments"

Lorna Wing (1981), a renowned researcher who is also the mother of an autistic daughter, came up with the phrase "The Triad of Impairments" to describe the chief areas of disability defining the autistic spectrum. As they are usually described, these are:

- Problems with social interaction and relationships;
- Problems with communication;
- Problems with imagination.

The last term is somewhat misleading, as it doesn't mean "lack of imagination" in a conventional sense. Some children and adults with Asperger's syndrome can be highly "imaginative" as the term is usually understood, developing elaborate fantasy worlds. Instead it's more useful to think of this element of the triad in terms of problems with flexible thinking, leading to problems coping with change and a need for rigid routines, and difficulty imagining what other people may be thinking.

I will briefly review the key features of Asperger's syndrome before examining each in greater detail in the context of its effects on school life.

The most conspicuous element of the triad in people with Asperger's syndrome is the one I have placed first: problems with social interaction. Because we mostly have apparently "normal" language, our communication difficulties are more subtle than the obvious ones of a person who does not speak or is echolalic. Instead, our difficulties often involve the aspects of language which go beyond literal meaning, such as recognizing sarcasm or metaphorical use of language. It is a cliché (but a true one) that a child with Asperger's, asked "Do you know what 6 times 7 is?" is quite likely to answer simply "yes" without realizing that this was not a factual enquiry but an instruction meaning "tell me what 6 times 7 is". Nor do we intuitively understand the use of language for social purposes – for example, it's hard for us to grasp that "How are you?" is not a request for information. Many children with Asperger's idea of a perfect conversation consists of their imparting a string of facts on a topic in which they are obsessively interested (the same is true for many adults with Asperger's, of course, even if we may have grudgingly come to accept that this is not true for everyone. I am very happy in that I have a number of friends who will permit me to talk at inordinate length about my latest obsession; sometimes I even succeed in conveying some of my fervour to them). The idea that conversation could have other functions is not a natural one for us. In this sense, our problems with communication are essentially social (rather than grammatical) in nature and so I will treat social and communicative problems together.

The essential social problem in autistic spectrum conditions is not one of avoidance of, or lack of interest in, interacting with others (although either of these may also be present since social interaction can seem at best pointless, at worst terrifying), but inability to grasp the tacit rules that govern social interaction intuitively, or to "read" the facial expression, tone of voice and body language of others. Often, our own body language is odd and we do not express emotions in the same way as others (I remember as a child that I had to teach myself how to do a "social smile" while looking in a mirror). Our voices are often flat or sing-song.

Many people with Asperger's syndrome, like me, spontaneously compare themselves to extraterrestrials – one woman on the Internet brilliantly describes autism as "Oops-wrong-planet" syndrome – or to humans on an alien planet (as in Temple Grandin's famous self-description as an "anthropologist on Mars"). Others find a kindred spirit in Star Trek's Mr. Spock, perpetually baffled by the illogical behaviour of humans, or his successor in Star Trek: The Next Generation, the literal-minded android Data.

Some researchers (e.g. Frith 1989) have argued that some characteristic autistic social and communicative problems can be understood in terms of a lack of "Theory of Mind"– the ability to conceive of others as having different beliefs and information from oneself, which neurotypical children develop early in life ("neurotypical", often abbreviated to NT, is a term coined by autistic people to describe the "so-called normal"). While most people fitting Asperger's description do develop the ability to pass tests of Theory of Mind, it has been suggested that we often do so at a later age, and certainly many people with Asperger's experienced problems during their school days involving failing to realize that other people didn't know everything that we did.

Before I was 9 or 10, I have almost no memories involving thinking about how others were perceiving me, to the extent that when looking back with this in mind I experience a constant sense of surprise. For example, I've always remembered that when I was bored in classes I used to lick my fingers and the palms of my hands, because I liked the taste of salt in my sweat, and stare at my hands for ages, which I also liked. I only realized recently that I must have been about 10 at the time I did this, and it occurred to me that this must have seemed very odd to other people. I simply never thought about it in that way before. I have one memory from that period of realising that someone had a trivially inaccurate belief about me, and being upset, because I felt you had to make sure people knew the truth. Other than this one instance, I don't have any memories at all of thinking spontaneously of how others would perceive me or react to my behaviour. In general, I must have behaved as if I thought I was invisible. This fits in very well with the "Theory of Mind" theory which some researchers have come up with, which suggests that autistic children have particular trouble thinking about and imagining what other people know.

Sometimes researchers describe this in terms of "lack of empathy", which is unfortunately misleading. They are using "empathy" in a very precise way to mean the ability to read other people's emotions and work out what they are thinking; this is **not** the same as "sympathy", the ability to **care** about what other people feel or think. People with autism can often seem self-absorbed and egocentric, but we're not selfish; we're not always very good at thinking about the impacts of our actions on others, but that doesn't mean we don't care. Sarah's description of herself at school age demonstrates the distinction:

> My desire to always be on good terms with others motivated me strongly to learn how to interact with others successfully. I would feel absolutely terrible if I did anything that disappointed someone or hurt someone's feelings. So I did have the ability to feel empathy and guilt; once in third grade, for instance, I cried uncontrollably after killing a few ants in my room. But what I lacked was an ability to predict how others would be affected by my actions (and inaction). I had difficulty seeing things from someone else's point of view. I found games involving strategy (such as chess, which someone tried to teach me in fifth grade) extremely difficult.

People with Asperger's are characteristically inflexible and have a great need for our personal routines (which may co-exist with apparent complete disorganization in other areas). Sarah remembered:

> I … learned the route my mom would drive to certain destinations, such as the store or school, and again if she deviated from the normal course of things I would get very upset. I would point out the window and say, 'We have to go down this street' …

At least in part because we can't use social understanding to predict and control the behaviour of others, we rely on things being predictable and events taking place exactly as we are told they will – the alternative is complete chaos. Many people with Asperger's become intolerably anxious if told something "might" happen, or fall apart completely if something we have been told "will" happen, doesn't. Surprises, even ostensibly pleasurable ones such as parties or presents, are usually extremely stressful for us. This rigidity, among other causes, may lead to very high anxiety levels and "explosive" behaviour. We often "perseverate", getting "stuck" on a particular response or question even when it is no longer useful, and may have difficulty planning ways of tackling a problem or shifting our attention from one topic to another.

Beyond the "triad"

Perhaps the most distinctive feature of Asperger's syndrome is the presence of obsessions or "special interests". Mostly, these involve collecting objects or facts on a particular topic:

> *From an early age, I developed narrow, all-encompassing interests and it has been difficult for me to be interested in two or more things at once. So I would usually rotate between interests, being obsessed with one subject for a month or two and then go back to other special interests. When I'm fascinated by something, I try to learn everything I can about it. These interests largely involved the rote memorization of facts. (Sarah)*

> *I would get in 'ruts' where I would only read about one thing for months and months – the earliest one I remember was water towers. I wanted to know everything there was about water towers. I wanted my dad to buy me one and pour out all the water so I could live at the top. (Michelle)*

Joseph hypothesized that:

> *While not all people with Asperger's syndrome are trainspotters, all trainspotters are almost indubitably people with Asperger's syndrome.*

The topics of obsessions can seem very bizarre to non-autistic people – real-life examples include water spirits, the etymology of place-names, national flags, nostrils and collecting dead light-bulbs (a one-time passion of mine). Nonetheless they are sources of great pleasure and delight and the objects for a pure passion of the intellect of an intensity which is surely rare among schoolchildren.

Almost all people on the autistic spectrum have sensory anomalies, possibly owing to problems in the cerebellum, which acts rather like a "volume knob" on the senses. These may include sensory hyper-sensitivities (where the volume on a particular sense is turned up too high – so that, for example, a light touch may be perceived as overwhelming), hypo-sensitivities (where the volume is too low so that, for example, pain from an injury is not registered) and processing problems. Processing problems include difficulty filtering out background stimuli and problems following a stimulus (for example, making sense of a long string of spoken instructions). Sometimes sensitivities may only be to certain ranges of stimuli – e.g. certain types of touch (often light, feathery touches) or certain frequencies of sound (I still have to leave the room if anyone uses a vacuum cleaner or a particular type of waste disposal unit). Many people have some of each type of problem, and sensory problems can also vary at different times, depending on how much else the person is trying to process and how overloaded by stimuli they are. The result of sensory anomalies can be apparently irrational aversions to everyday objects:

> I can barely stand the feel or sound of EXPANDED POLYSTYRENE (the white foam used in packaging). (David Hawker)

They can also result in preoccupations with objects which produce pleasant sensations:

> I recall when I was 6, I sometimes licked hand railings at school with my tongue because I liked their metallic smoothness and coolness. (Sarah)

It is very common for people with Asperger's to avoid eye contact, finding it uncomfortable, and to be unable to use it to send or receive social signals. Equally common is tactile defensiveness, where physical contact or even the physical proximity of others is experienced as overwhelming and intolerable. This can cause problems of misinterpretation on both sides – when a child wails "she hit me!" after a teacher pats them on the head or a classmate accidentally brushes against them in the corridor, they are likely to be seen as lying or exaggerating, and it is hard for others to understand that they may be stating their perceptions accurately, while it may be equally hard for the child with Asperger's to understand that the hurt was not intentional.

Many researchers have suggested that people with Asperger's syndrome are characteristically clumsy and awkward. Often, we may combine very poor gross motor control with relatively good fine motor control. Usually, "stereotyped movements" such as hand-flapping and rocking are less common in people with Asperger's than they are in more severely autistic people, but many people do have them, while others have more subtle mannerisms like repetitive pacing or carrying the hands at chest height. While researchers still debate the nature and function of such "stereotypies", people with Asperger's are unanimous in agreeing that they have a positive self-regulatory function, usually serving to express excitement or soothe anxiety. I can only describe it by saying that they help me think. It is possible to learn to suppress such movements when necessary, but this requires significant effort and usually causes a lot of tension.

Typically, people with Asperger's have an unusual learning style: intensely concrete rather than abstract, absorbed in details while having significant difficulty perceiving overall "gestalts", and suited to processing information organized spatially rather than temporally (I will examine the classroom implications of this at greater length later in the book). Often, what is "obvious" to us is very difficult for others to grasp, while we have equal trouble understanding what neurotypical people take to be obvious.

Recently, some researchers (notably Frith and Happé 1994) have suggested that the manner in which information is processed by the brain may be at the root of many autistic difficulties – and strengths. They argue that neurotypical processing of information is dominated by a drive for central coherence which pulls bits of information together to derive overall patterns and meanings. In contrast, autistic processing of information does not pull information together to such a strong degree, resulting both in weaknesses when it comes to contextual understanding and seeing the "big picture", and in greater accuracy in perceiving details and greater ability in tasks which require one to separate out bits of information, such as the "block design" and "embedded figures" cognitive tests. More colloquially: people with autism are unable to see the wood for the trees but we see the individual trees in very great detail.

This theory – the "weak central coherence" theory – helps make sense of many of the problems in comprehension and in perception of relevance which I will describe later in the book.

This idiosyncratic way of processing information and learning may be linked to the fact that we often have very uneven developmental profiles, combining remarkable abilities in one area with severe problems in another. IQ tests often show scores that are well below normal on some sub-tests and off the top of the chart in others (for a minority of people with autistic spectrum conditions, this uneven profile is extreme enough to create "savant" and "splinter" skills).

This often causes confusion among teachers who may be unable to believe that a child who achieves effortlessly in one subject may genuinely be unable to cope with another. It is not uncommon for one subject teacher to see a child as "gifted" while another sees them as "backward" or "difficult" – at the time I started primary school, my parents simultaneously received recommendations from different quarters that I should be sent to a school for gifted children, and that I should be sent to an educational psychologist because of my "problem" behaviour (including pacing up and down the classroom and failing to respond to instructions given to the class as a whole – years later, the teacher in question explained to my mother that I had been behaving "just like an autistic child"). Attempts to classify a child as one or the other often run into difficulties:

Academically, the teachers saw me as 'gifted', but I could never pass some of the dumb spatial orientation questions and arrangement of odd shaped beads on the enrichment test … (Fred)

Despite academic ability in certain areas, "life skills" may need to be explicitly taught. I didn't start mastering many "daily living skills" until I was in my mid-to-late teens, including being able to cross a road on my own without waiting for hours until there were no cars visible anywhere (crossing roads is difficult as my depth perception problems mean I find it almost impossible to judge how fast things are coming towards me), and it was also at about this age that I finally learnt how to buy something in a shop.

Beyond "impairments"

It is important not to see Asperger's syndrome solely in terms of impairments: as nothing more than a cluster of handicaps. In contrast to the common picture of an "autistic shell", people with Asperger's syndrome often define autism as a "way of being", something that is a deep and fundamental part of who we are. As researchers from Hans Asperger himself onwards have noted, the unusual ways of thinking and perceiving the world which are at the core of Asperger's syndrome may be uniquely valuable; indeed, Asperger wrote:

Able autistic individuals can rise to eminent positions and perform with such outstanding success that one may even conclude that only such people are capable of certain achievements …Their unswerving determination and penetrating intellectual powers, part of their spontaneous and original mental activity, their narrowness and single-mindedness, as manifested in their special interests, can be immensely valuable and can lead to outstanding achievements in their chosen areas. (1991, p. 88)

Researcher Tony Attwood (1997) records that one of the people with Asperger's syndrome whom he met (tantalizingly un-named) was "a retired professor who was awarded the Nobel Prize", and Christopher Gillberg, the Swedish expert on autism and Asperger's syndrome, has suggested that Ludwig Wittgenstein, thought by many to be the greatest philosopher of the twentieth century, had Asperger's syndrome. Attwood emphasizes that: "the thinking is different, potentially highly original, often misunderstood, but is not defective." (1997, p. 126)

The problems arise, not so much from Asperger's syndrome itself, as from a social world which is not designed for people with Asperger's syndrome but for people who think and perceive the world in very different ways.

Myths and misinformation

It is necessary to note that misinformation and myths about the autistic spectrum are widespread; it is still common for people with Asperger's syndrome and our families to encounter someone who has a vague memory, dating from a book they read in the 60s or 70s that "autism is caused by refrigerator mothers" or that "autistic people don't have emotions". Many of us have come across "You can't be autistic, you can talk" or "You can't be autistic, I've seen *Rainman* and you're nothing like that". Even when a piece of knowledge is accurate, as always, a little knowledge is a dangerous thing; the statements that "people with autism have no imagination" or "don't have empathy" are often misunderstood in ways which are clearly counter-productive.

Misinformation (and in some cases, deliberate fraud) are even more widespread on the topic of educational techniques and "cures". Ever since autism was first defined in the 40s, claims of "miracle cures" have been proclaimed every few years, and not one has ever been substantiated; in fact, many of them have actually done considerable harm both to children and to their parents (see Howlin 1998, chapter 4).

The Internet is particularly problematic in this respect: it's a wonderful tool for communication and connecting people (especially people with Asperger's, as we often find it much easier to communicate without the confusing elements of body language, tone of voice, or pressure to reply in real time), but it's essential to remember that anyone can put anything on the net that they like. Unless it comes, for example, from a recognized medical department or university, there are no guarantees of its reliability at all. There are plenty of deliberate deceptions and hoaxes and also many people passing on, in good faith, information which is dangerously inaccurate.

When it comes to headline-making claims of "cures", current research evidence seems clear: autistic spectrum conditions are rooted in complex neurological differences for which it is impossible to imagine any quick fix. It is possible to teach many skills and dramatically improve the overall functioning of someone on the spectrum, but we still remain qualitatively different, perhaps achieving some of the same things as neurotypical people but by very different routes. Even those people with Asperger's who are able to pass for "normal-if-a-bit-eccentric" experience the world in radically different ways.

Because the e-mail list I run focuses on university issues, the hundreds of people with autistic spectrum conditions with whom I am in touch include people who are probably among the most high-functioning and successful autistic people in the world – people with degrees, people with PhDs, people holding down jobs, even two people who are married. Not one of these people result from any of the supposed "miracle cure" treatments or educational programmes and not one of them is in any way "cured". I have never ever met anyone with autism who has become "normal" and consequently I advise extreme scepticism with respect to claims of "cures". There are plenty of educational techniques and tips that are genuinely helpful, but they're not glamorous, they don't pretend to be "cures" and so they tend not to make the headlines.

Undiagnosed Asperger's

Unless a child has had language problems sufficient to earn them a diagnosis of autism already, Asperger's syndrome is typically not diagnosed until a child is at least school age (and it is usually school problems that trigger a referral). Many children remain undiagnosed for years. Christopher Gillberg has suggested that over a third of all adults with Asperger's are never evaluated or correctly diagnosed (Bauer, not dated). Therefore, although the incidence of Asperger's syndrome makes it likely that every teacher will encounter at least one pupil with Asperger's during their teaching career, it is quite possible that they will not have that label attached. Asperger's syndrome, like the rest of the autistic spectrum and like many other neurological conditions, is much more common in boys than in girls, but there are also indications that girls with Asperger's may be particularly likely to go undiagnosed.

Once one becomes familiar with Asperger's syndrome, it is often startlingly easy to spot, being highly distinctive. As Peeters and Gillberg comment, "Once considered, the diagnosis of Asperger syndrome is not generally a difficult one. The problem is that it is often not taken into consideration." (1999, p. 34)

Sometimes children with Asperger's get through their school days without any sort of label except informal ones such as "odd", "weird" or, more kindly, "eccentric". In other cases, their problems will be seen as resulting from conditions such as attention-deficit/hyperactivity disorder, giftedness, dyspraxia or dyslexia. In some cases, these diagnoses may be correct (many people with Asperger's qualify for a "dual diagnosis") but they are insufficient to explain all the problems the person in question experiences, and fail to point teachers towards a correct understanding of the nature and causes of the problem; individual problems, such as with hand-writing or maths, may be treated in isolation, while the overall picture is overlooked and the child continues to be blamed for being "rude", "stand-offish" and so on. David A. commented:

There were loads of problems identified, but nothing was ever taken seriously enough for it to be useful to me ...

In other cases, children with Asperger's receive misdiagnoses which are at best unhelpful and confusing and at worst lead to their receiving "help" which is actually inappropriate and damaging: this occurs when a child is mistakenly labelled as "emotionally disturbed" or as having an "antisocial personality disorder", as some people I talked to were. David A., who now has a diagnosis of Asperger's syndrome, was actually diagnosed at the age of 13 with schizophrenia.

Despite the common reluctance to "label" children, which I will discuss in the next chapter, it is vital that Asperger's syndrome be accurately diagnosed as early as possible. Teachers are in a key position to identify possible signs of undiagnosed Asperger's and help set the bureaucratic wheels in motion to obtain a referral to a clinician.

3

"We are not broken": Asperger's syndrome and the goals of education

> ... we do things in different ways [but] we are of the same worth and value and we are not broken and do not need to be 'fixed' or 'cured'.
> (Jean-Paul Bovee, personal communication)

Before discussing the school experience of children with Asperger's, it is necessary to point out that teachers, parents and people with Asperger's may have very different assumptions and ideas about what school is *for* and that these very different conceptions of education and its goals have a marked impact on the education that a child receives. Is Asperger's syndrome a "label", to be avoided? Should education aim to "normalize" children with Asperger's? Should all children be included in the mainstream? In these debates, the voices of the people being discussed often go unheard, and the particular needs of children with Asperger's, as distinct from disabled children in general, are rarely considered. In this chapter, I will try to articulate some of the experiences and feelings of people with Asperger's syndrome on these topics, and in doing so, express heretical opinions on three particularly controversial issues: labelling, normalization and inclusion (in writing this chapter, I have drawn extensively on the experiences and opinions of many other people with Asperger's, but obviously the views I express are my own and I do not claim to speak for all people with Asperger's).

Labelling?

I've noticed that parents, teachers and other professionals are often reluctant to seek a diagnosis of Asperger's, or to talk openly about a child's diagnosis, for fear of "labelling" them. On the basis of my own experiences and those of others, I think that this reluctance is deeply misguided and actively harmful to children with Asperger's.

Finally getting the right label was one of the best things that has ever happened to me. By my teens I was seriously depressed after years of being different and not knowing why, and believing that, since no-one gave a name to my problem, I must just be imagining it, or not trying hard enough (after a decade of trying very hard and failing very hard, to be like everyone else). This experience was shared by many other people with Asperger's.

Some people are afraid that having a label will stigmatize a child. But social stigma is attached to being disabled or different in any way, not to the label itself (this process can be seen at work in the shift from "mental retardation" to "mental handicap" to "learning difficulties", as each term in turn became contaminated by stigma). Sadly, someone who is different will be stigmatized whether they have a label or not, and children with Asperger's who escape official labelling generally don't escape unofficial labelling. When I didn't have an official diagnostic label my teachers unofficially labelled me as "emotionally disturbed", "rude" and so on and my classmates unofficially labelled me "weirdo", "nerd" and "freak"; frankly, I prefer the official label. It's the stigma that's attached to being different which is the problem, not the label.

Similarly, if a label is used to pigeonhole a child, overlooking their individual needs and abilities in favour of an Identi-Kit picture of "children with Asperger's syndrome", that's clearly wrong. But, again, it's the pigeonholing that's the problem, not the label.

Avoiding the label doesn't make the differences go away. Someone with undiagnosed Asperger's still has Asperger's. Sometimes parents in particular will react as if the diagnosis itself has harmed their child, and that if they could only get the diagnosis reversed, their child's problems would go away.

But the right "label" is simply a way of *describing* someone which allows people to understand their differences better. Speech and language therapist Maureen Aarons has suggested that the diagnosis of autism is best seen as a context, a framework within which a child's difficulties and strengths can be understood: the question "does this child have autism?" can be re-phrased as "do this child's problems and behaviour make sense in the context of autism?"

A label may reveal problems, but it also provides the tools needed to understand and begin coping with, those problems. Obviously, a label is the key to a child's getting any special educational resources and support that they need, but even for those few children with Asperger's who can manage in a mainstream school without additional help, a label is the key to understanding (and in chapter 9, I will discuss the importance of a diagnosis of Asperger's in developing *self*-understanding).

Shying away from a label simply reinforces the perception that having a disability is shameful, embarrassing, something that must be "hushed up" if the person in question is to be treated as an equal (imagine the response if someone announced that the solution to racism in schools was to "avoid labelling children as black").

In some cases, the desire not to "label" children actually seems to stem from a denial that they have genuine disabilities, and a belief that they are somehow making excuses or trying to claim benefits to which they are not entitled: just as dyslexia is still sometimes cruelly maligned as "middle-class for thick", so I have heard Asperger's syndrome described as "just a fancy term for 'shy'".

Normalization?

The desire to avoid "labelling" is often linked to a belief in normalization. Although there seems to be a vague consensus that normalization is "a good thing", the term in fact has very different (sometimes opposing) meanings attached to it.

It is sometimes used to refer to the right of disabled people to have an ordinary life (for example, to live in a home, with staff to provide support if necessary, rather than a hospital), with opportunities equal to those taken for granted by non-disabled people.

It has also been used (by proponents such as Wolf Wolfensberger) to mean the "utilization of means which are as culturally normative as possible, in order to establish and/or maintain personal behaviors and characteristics which are as culturally normative as possible" (Wolfensberger, quoted in Brown and Smith (1992), p. 4). In the latter case, the assumption is that people with disabilities will not be valued or accepted by society unless they behave in ways which society deems valuable and acceptable: in other words, "act normal." The priority of the teacher or professional, then, is to make the disabled person act in a way which improves their public "image", regardless of their needs or choices (Wolfensberger advocates "systematic and long term reinforcement for emitting the desired responses", ibid., p. 12). He specifies, among other things, that the person should "walk with a normal gait ... use normal movements and normal expressive behavior patterns ... dress like other persons of his age" (p. 103) and seems to suggest that adaptive strategies that increase a person's ability to function should be rejected if they are visibly "abnormal": "wearing a hearing aid may be a greater obstacle to finding and keeping a job than being hard of hearing" (p. 104). Indeed, anything which might "label" the person in question as disabled is to be avoided.

This philosophy, unsurprisingly, has increasingly been criticized from a disability-rights standpoint. As Sue Szivos (1992) argues, "while it purports to revalue people with disabilities, [normalization] is rooted in a hostility to and denial of 'differentness'." (Szivos, p. 126). Instead of starting with the needs, choices and values of a disabled individual, it starts with the unchallenged standards of "normal" people (with who is and what is "normal" also left unchallenged). "Normal" people may take it as a basic human right to be accepted as they are; the rest of us are viewed only in terms of what will make us more acceptable to them.

Far from seeming radical or positive, the philosophy of normalization seems painfully familiar to those of us whose very disability lies in our "differentness". Most of us have already spent years being taught that who we are is fundamentally wrong and in need of "cure" and having others (whether parents or teachers or other professionals) try to force us again and again to do what we *cannot* do – that is, be "normal":

I hate to tell you that people with autism cannot conform to what they are not. I've been there, done that and don't want to ever do it again!!! (Jean-Paul)

In schools, the impulse of teachers to try to make children with Asperger's behave in a "normal" way often leads to a concentration on "treating" harmless differences at the expense of actually educating the child in question. Teachers are unwilling to accommodate autistic styles of learning; instead, all too often, when children develop strategies for themselves that increase their ability to learn and cope (such as pacing in order to think, or making drawings or talking to themselves in class in order to follow the lesson), teachers promptly suppress them as "inappropriate" (and are then unable to understand why the child fails to learn or exhibits "challenging behaviour"):

They would not let me play with the colored wood blocks because those were for the primary kids. But I was greatly attracted to the bright colors. Maybe if they had tried to teach me with bright colored manipulatives, even though I was older than the age they thought should be playing with them, I might have learned a little more about math. (Jack)

Autistic writer and advocate Jim Sinclair argues that "a common experience of many people with a variety of different disabilities is that a goal of looking and acting 'as normal as possible' is often achieved at the expense of being able to function as well as possible with one's disability. Adapting, accommodating and coping with disability often requires learning to do things differently from the ways nondisabled people do them." (Sinclair 1998)

Seeing children with Asperger's only in terms of deficits and deviations from the norm typically leads to an exclusive focus on attempting to remedy weaknesses, instead of developing strengths:

My strengths were taken for granted and they rubbed my nose into my problems relentlessly. (Darius)

In contrast, Gary Mesibov and Victoria Shea (not dated) of the TEACCH programme have argued that autism can in many ways be seen as a culture, complete with its own ways of understanding the world, communicating and so on. They explain that, since the neurological basis of autism cannot be altered:

> *… we do not take 'being normal' as the goal of our educational and therapeutic efforts. Rather, the long-term goal of the TEACCH programme is for the student with autism to fit as well as possible into our society as an adult. We achieve this goal by respecting the differences that the autism creates within each student and working within his or her culture to teach the skills needed to function within our society.*

In support of this, everyone with Asperger's I spoke to agreed that we learnt best when teaching works with, rather than against, our idiosyncratic learning styles and interests (indeed, many people were only able to learn at all when this was so). Obsessive interests, however obscure, could be used to motivate and power learning and an effective strategy was allowing the child to specialize initially in the area of their interests and strengths before expanding outwards into more general knowledge and, where necessary, tackling weaknesses:

> *The chance to specialise first and then generalise would have taught me better how to generalise rather than the way it's done … (David A.)*

It is clearly important to inform children with Asperger's about social rules so that they can make informed choices about how to behave; however, it must also be recognized that while outrageous social blunders may be avoided, people with Asperger's will never be "normal" and we should not be expected to be. If we are to learn successfully, we need our teachers to adjust to our autistic styles of learning; if we are to survive psychologically, we need those around us to acknowledge and respect who we are, instead of viewing us only in relation to a standard of a "normality" which, by definition, we will never attain. Research by Susan Solursh (1999) suggests that successful adult outcome, particularly when it comes to developing a positive self-concept, may be made more likely by parental acceptance of - as opposed to attempts to "cure" – autistic spectrum conditions and I believe that the attitudes of teachers and other professionals are likely to be equally influential.

Energy should be conserved for dealing with problems which are *intrinsically* distressing or disabling, as opposed to aspects of a person's behaviour or learning style which are just "different". The goal of education should be enabling the child to learn in the way that they learn best and develop the skills needed to navigate through an alien world, rather than enforcing "normality" at any cost.

Inclusion?

"Full inclusion" (the belief that *all* disabled children should be placed in mainstream schools) has become something of a dogma, despite the fact that a number of groups of people with disabilities, notably the Deaf, have protested against it (see chapter 4, "The Least Restrictive Environment", in Cohen 1995, or chapter 16, "The Education of Deaf Children", by Harlan Lane, in Kauffman and Hallahan 1995). Yet, as with normalization, there are aspects of the philosophy of full inclusion which are remarkably conservative and aspects of its practice which can be singularly damaging to children with Asperger's syndrome. As Jim Sinclair (1998) notes, many in the disability community are concerned that "involuntary inclusion is as problematic as involuntary segregation."

Inclusion for children with autistic spectrum conditions is often promoted on the grounds that "normal" peers will model "appropriate" behaviour for the child with autism (leaving aside the fact that one of the notable elements of autistic spectrum conditions is our inability to absorb social conventions from our environment), while contact with other autistic children might encourage the development of "bad" (i.e. autistic) behaviours (I am unable to help wondering occasionally whether people advocating these views actually harbour an unconscious belief that autism is contagious). As Jim Sinclair notes, "stressing the importance of contact with certain peers just because those peers are not disabled conveys the unmistakable message that disabled people are undesirable as peers" (Sinclair 1998).

Much of the literature on full inclusion focuses on the role of school as an environment for socializing. Questions of whether a particular child is receiving an optimal education in the mainstream environment are often brushed aside in favour of the benefits that will supposedly accrue to them simply through interacting with and being part of a classroom with "normal" children (sometimes, often in cases involving children with profound and multiple disabilities, there seems to be a tacit assumption that they are not expected to learn anything anyway and so it doesn't matter if their learning is not optimized as long as they get to interact with "normal" children).

This emphasis on socialization as the main purpose of school is obviously going to have very different implications for those of us whose primary disability is a social one (imagine the implications for children who use wheelchairs of a theory which took team sports as the primary purpose of school). The assumption that "social integration" is an uncomplicated benefit and even the primary goal of inclusion may result in a situation in which the needs of children with autistic spectrum conditions are completely overlooked.

The perspective of children with Asperger's is a very different one: typically, we see school as a place for learning things (not unreasonably, given that this is how school is usually explained to children), and find it extremely hard to mix academic learning with social interaction. Other children often figure in our picture of the world chiefly as obstacles to our learning:

> I don't know for the life of me why a school at all needed to be associated [with] academic learning. I was good at academics and motivation was never a problem for me. I worked very well on my own – even still now I am described as industrious. I was an idiot socially. Mixing academics with social peer interaction was a recipe to ensure I'd fail at both. Perhaps it might have been a good idea to work on these separately so that one didn't have to spill over into the other and mess me up. It also would have allowed for my level of achievement to be different academically than socially and I might have developed better self-esteem. As it turned out, I reached a point (which I still am at) where I can't see that I can do anything right. (Alice)

Having noted the problems inherent in theories of "full inclusion", it may be possible to try to take a clear look at what the experiences of children with Asperger's syndrome are in different placements.

Generic "special needs" schools or classes which were designed for children with learning difficulties or other delays, or which mixed children with a wide variety of special needs, were invariably experienced as unsatisfactory.

This was not because of prejudice or difficulty relating to children with learning difficulties and other disabilities: in fact, many people found that their first and only friendships were with other disabled children, who were much easier to understand than "normal" classmates. Sarah reported: "I did connect a little … with some of the kids … (particularly a girl who had brain damage from suffocation and two autistic boys, both of whom were in my class) … On the other hand, "normal" kids … would often get me upset." (My first friend ever – and for a long while my only friend – was a non-verbal autistic girl who was the daughter of a colleague of my mum's.) Indeed, a few people I interviewed were working or training as special needs assistants, speech and language therapists, learning disability nurses, psychologists, etc. and hoping to work specifically with children and adults with autism and other disabilities.

The chief objection was that such placements simply failed to provide for the academic abilities of children with Asperger's, let alone stimulate them:

> I was put in what were euphemistically called special classes. It insulted the heck out of me because all of my classmates were 'slow' and I was not. I was rarely challenged and spent much time doing busy work while my classmates learned. (Richard)

In high school I was put into at least one 'easy' class (where all the kids did was to hand-copy into a notebook from a science textbook). (Jack)

… in grades 7 and 8 I was put into what was considered 'special education.' In this class, my exceptional skills in mathematics were ignored and I was forced to do mathematics many years below my ability. Special education for my reading disability meant that I continually re-read simple books meant for much younger children and the alphabet, which I had not yet learned. (Schuyler)

(It should be noted that children in mainstream classrooms sometimes also ended up being given "make work" or "busy work", either because they could not keep up with the rest of the class on a given topic or because they had already completed the work that the rest of the class were still struggling with; the same boredom and frustration resulted.)

Simply providing slower or more basic teaching failed to address the learning needs of children with Asperger's, even in subjects in which they were delayed. One person commented, regarding remedial maths classes, that:

The extra lessons didn't do much good because they didn't address my real problems. Teachers assumed that I didn't understand maths, but I could explain the nature of the particular math-problem better than they themselves and I had no problem with the analytical thought processes. Numbers simply don't mean anything to me. The reasoning was not the problem but the actual sums were. A lot of remedial teaching was wasted on me because people assumed that I was having the same kind of problems retarded kids have. (Darius)

Meanwhile, the social problems of Asperger's syndrome were not addressed, even though these were often the reason why the child had been placed in a special class or school in the first place:

My social deficit is quite distinct and significant and yet no remediation was provided in this area. (Schuyler)

Mixing together children with a great variety of special needs could also expose children with Asperger's to possible manipulation and victimization by emotionally and behaviourally disturbed children. Most importantly, it was clear that the only common denominator amongst these children was that the mainstream classrooms didn't want them. They were being placed to meet the system's needs, not their own, and their status as second-class citizens, rejected and stigmatized, was very clear:

…it was decided that I more fit the category of 'emotionally disturbed' (ED) than 'learning disabled' and I was bussed to another district 'to

*better meet my needs' in an ED class there. The bus was the nightmare
of my life. Tossed together were developmentally disabled kids, 'mentally
retarded' kids, major big time behavior challenges of kids, ADD/ADHD
kids, plain vanilla emotionally disturbed kids – some of these were
teenagers – and me. We were all together in this circus tent being sent
somewhere, we felt, because we were so defective that even our home
districts couldn't deal with us, and this was manifested in the rage, the
fights and obscenities that were a regular part of the ride. (Karen)*

The only plus of generic "special" classes noted was that sometimes
staff shortages and overwork meant that a student with AS would be left alone
and allowed to teach themselves:

*What my somewhat overworked teachers (20–25 kids in a special
school) did for me was to leave me alone and provide supplies. (Helen)*

However, it was not clear that mainstream classrooms were much
better. Many people commented on the damaging effects of being "dumped" in
a mainstream classroom, often without understanding or support, and Karen also
wrote:

*Even if I did get tested and evaluated to death, and develop something of
a phobia of these tests as a result … at least, that's better in some ways
than being stuck in a typical classroom and in effect told to 'sink or swim'.*

Even when a child had been formally diagnosed, mainstream teachers
usually had no, or minimal, knowledge of Asperger's syndrome. It is important to
emphasize that merely reading a pamphlet or going to a one-day workshop,
while helpful, is not enough to ensure an adequate understanding; as Peeters and
Gillberg comment, "What would you say if you had lung problems but were
being treated by a dentist ('Oh, but we shall be sending him to a lung congress')."
(1999, p. 81) Typically, non-teaching staff (such as dinner ladies), who often dealt
with the child in many difficult situations outside the classroom, were given no
information on Asperger's at all.

Victimization and bullying – including by teachers – were extremely
common and I will cover them in greater detail later.

Perhaps the greatest problem is the assumption that the mainstream
classroom is somehow neutral and not specialized. From the perspective of
someone with Asperger's, it becomes clear that the mainstream classroom is in
fact very specifically designed to meet the needs of children who learn in
neurotypical ways: it's not mainstream at all, but "normalstream". Because of this
assumption, however, there is a pervasive failure to acknowledge the ways in
which a classroom, although physically accessible, may still be impossible for a
given child to access in any meaningful way. Jim Sinclair comments that "For

people whose disabilities involve significant sensory issues, as autism does, inclusive environments are often nightmares of continual sensory bombardment which interferes with learning and causes constant discomfort or pain." (Sinclair 1998). The way in which lessons were taught and the classroom was organized also often rendered the classroom cognitively inaccessible: Darius remembered "… my class was a terrible experience for any HFA/AS kid. Too noisy and unstructured." In some cases, enough adaptations can be made to make lessons accessible for a child with Asperger's, but in other cases the changes necessary would render the classroom intolerably barren and boring by the standards of the neurotypical pupils.

Mainstreaming with an aide can sometimes work, but can also end up with an (untrained) aide teaching the child while the rest of the class get on with their work with the teacher: the child is integrated only by being physically present in the same classroom with the other children, while missing out on having a trained teacher, let alone one with specialist knowledge of Asperger's.

One particularly painful aspect of mainstreaming is isolation from other children with Asperger's. Many people reached adulthood without ever having met anybody like themselves, each believing that they were the "only one" (and for many people, just learning that they were not "the only one" was a key benefit of diagnosis). I think this degree of isolation is very hard for neurotypical people even to imagine. My non-verbal autistic friend was the only person I had ever met who seemed normal to me and, as I have already described, the idea that there might be more people somewhere in the universe who were *like me* was the stuff of my most secret childhood longings and fantasies. This pervasive isolation makes it extremely difficult for children with Asperger's to develop a positive identity and sense of themselves as disabled people.

On a practical level, I never had the chance to see other people make the same social mistakes as me, or to try to make friends on a "level playing field". Had I done so, I might have judged my own failures less harshly, and been more able to develop coping strategies to deal with them.

On an emotional level, the right to be average, not always to be the odd one out, is rarely considered – Jim Sinclair quotes Donna Williams as saying that "normal is being in the company of others like oneself." (Sinclair 1998). More than one person with Asperger's spontaneously and pointedly put "peers" in quotations marks when referring to their neurotypical schoolmates and almost everyone agreed that the chance to meet other children with Asperger's would have been extremely valuable to them (the only exception was one person who felt that he would not have taken up such an opportunity at the time because of his own unhappiness with his diagnosis and wish to avoid having anything to do with it).

For those who cannot cope in mainstream, a specialist school for students with Asperger's seems to be an obvious solution. I didn't get a chance to interview anyone on their experience of such schools, because no-one had been to one. Even nowadays, there are barely a handful of schools in existence which specialize in academically able children with autistic spectrum conditions; most schools for autistic children focus on the needs of those children who also have learning difficulties or who, for whatever reason, are unable to cope with academic work at a mainstream level (and it must be noted that there are still far too few of *these* schools to meet existing needs). As Patricia Howlin points out (1998, p. 240), the small size of most autistic schools, while in others respects an advantage, limits the range of academic provision they can offer: "If they have pupils with particular skills in maths, computing or even Greek, few autistic schools will have staff qualified enough in these topics to offer children the opportunity to take external examinations."

Children with Asperger's seem to "fall between two stools", with those who can cope academically in mainstream being put into mainstream to sink or swim, regardless of whether they can cope socially, and special school placement being considered only after a child has "failed" in mainstream, sometimes by having a nervous breakdown and/or developing clinical depression.

Different people with Asperger's syndrome have different opinions about what would have benefited them personally. Some felt that their mainstream placement could have worked well if only teachers had understood their needs and been willing to adapt. David Hawker wrote:

> *I don't see any major problems with the school. Just perhaps some allowances made in certain lessons – and educated, understanding teachers.*

Others felt that a mainstream placement would not have worked for them under any circumstances. Therese Joliffe, a woman with high-functioning autism, wrote:

> *Although ordinary schooling enabled me to leave with a dozen or so O-levels and a few A-levels and then to obtain a degree, it was not worth all the misery I suffered. (Joliffe, 1992, p. 13)*

As well as the obvious need for greater provision of special schools and units specifically for those pupils who can cope academically but not socially at a mainstream level, there is also considerable room for imaginative adaptations of existing provisions. For example, some schools specializing in specific learning difficulties (such as dyslexia and dyspraxia), or small, structured schools, might be able to adapt without too much difficulty to suit a student with Asperger's. Specialist autistic schools could be brought in as "consultants" to teachers working with children with Asperger's in mainstream schools and support groups, pen-pal schemes and e-mail lists could prevent isolation by linking pupils with Asperger's in mainstream. Conversely, autistic schools might be able to pool resources to bring in outside tutors where a pupil in an autistic school has high academic ability in a particular area. For some children with Asperger's, home tutoring or distance learning might work well.

There also needs to be acknowledgement that a child's needs may change markedly over time. For some children, a period of specialist schooling early on can help provide them with the skills necessary to thrive in a mainstream school; conversely, some may be able to survive in a mainstream school at primary age, but not at secondary age ("the age," as Joseph put it, "when the hormones start kicking in and kids become really vicious and/or miserable"), when peers may become markedly less tolerant of social abnormality. Movement back and forth between special and mainstream schools and dual placements (where a child may be primarily based at one school but also visit another, e.g. for social skills lessons), should be made easier.

There is much that can and should be learnt from the inclusion movement. No child should be segregated simply because they have a disability, nor should integration have to be "earned" by having only a mild disability or not requiring any additional support or adjustments to the classroom. Special schools must be integrated into society, rather than isolated from it, and cannot be allowed to function as "dumping grounds" providing disabled children with a second-class education.

All students with Asperger's syndrome need teachers who have a detailed knowledge of Asperger's and an educational environment in which they can participate meaningfully. For some students, this can be provided within a mainstream school; for others it can't. Decisions must be made on the basis of the individual's needs and preferences, not on the basis of dogma.

The goal of education for students with disabilities must be the provision of the best possible education and school experience and integration as equals into society. For some, inclusion in a mainstream school is a good way of achieving this goal – but it is a means not an end and when the two conflict, the end, not the means, should be given priority.

4

In the Classroom: the learning environment

The social classroom

Paradoxically, one of the major obstacles to learning for children with Asperger's syndrome is that we fail to see the classroom as anything other than a learning environment. We are oblivious to its social context and the problems this causes can greatly complicate learning in the classroom setting. For example, many people with Asperger's are liable to unconsciously "odd" behaviour, especially when absorbed in thought:

> I am … prone to 'laughing at nothing'. If I imagine or remember something funny I can laugh out loud. People at school complained about this during lessons, accusing me of laughing at nothing, then the teacher had to try and defend me … (David Hawker)

> I made noises when I got emotional, especially when I daydream. This made it hard because people were always demanding that I control myself … (Richard)

This is the sort of behaviour which can lead to children being seen as "in a world of their own" (it is worth noting that we are not in a separate world at all – just paying attention to very different aspects of this one):

> In second grade, I sat in the back of the classroom at a table by myself and on a few occasions, I took off my socks and put them on my hands as puppets and would talk and giggle to them. But once I began crying uncontrollably and when my teacher asked me what the problem was, I told her that my socks had 'died'. This struck her as rather bizarre. (Sarah)

Laughing at one's own thoughts could cause particular problems if another child was simultaneously being mischievous; the child with Asperger's could easily be blamed for "encouraging" behaviour of which they had been happily oblivious. Similarly, making noises or grimacing could be misunderstood as deliberately being "silly", "immature" or trying to make other children laugh. I was once severely told off for making faces at lunch, when in fact I had been reading recently about how Arctic explorers needed to do this to prevent frostbite (I was not able to explain this to my teacher at the time).

Many teachers immediately run up against the fact that children with Asperger's have no intuitive grasp of social hierarchy, a feature which is all too often mistaken for disobedience or disrespectfulness (the relationship between teachers and pupils with Asperger's syndrome will be discussed in much greater detail later). Asperger noted of the children he studied that: "They treat everyone as an equal as a matter of course ... They may demand a service or simply start a conversation on a theme of their own choosing. All this goes, of course, without any regard for differences in age, social rank or common courtesies." (Asperger, p. 81). Darius remembered "I had (and still have) a hard time interpreting what exactly is required. What are 'hard expectations one has to comply with' and what is optional? Other people seem to have no difficulties with that." We do not intend to be disrespectful – indeed we may be desperate to avoid displeasing others – but it does not occur to us that we are supposed to treat someone in a different, special way, just because they are a teacher. So a child with Asperger's may not understand that they are supposed to obey the teacher without discussion, let alone that they are not allowed to correct the teacher's errors (even though the teacher corrects theirs all the time):

> In my first week ... I got the schedule down pat and threw a tantrum if the teacher did something at 10 a.m. which was supposed to happen at 11 a.m. I would tell her, 'You're not supposed to do this now' and, after a while, she got tired of me telling her what to do. (Sarah)

Things are made worse by the reluctance of many teachers and others to make explicit many of the tacit rules of the classroom (for example, that one is expected to laugh at the teacher's jokes), and their tendency to supply principles which, if actually obeyed, land one instantly in trouble; Elizabeth reflected ruefully:

> When I was younger I used to take the little sayings parents and teachers told kids to heart ('don't lie', 'be yourself', etc) and really didn't understand that that wasn't actually what they wanted.

We may refuse to "take on trust" what the teacher says if it doesn't make sense to us or doesn't accord with our observations. Teachers are unlikely to get away with attempts to gloss over material deemed too difficult or inappropriate for a certain age group:

Some of the problems with math I was experiencing had to do with the fact that I was way beyond the level of ordinary kids in analytical reasoning. In primary, a lot of math problems and solutions are glossed over or simply not addressed at that level. If you see all sorts of implications when trying to solve a problem where you are not supposed to see them, let alone solve them, you may have a serious problem when trying to answer problems that are too simple. (Darius)

The point of things like exams may not be clear. Unless it is explicitly stated, pupils with Asperger's may not realize that the point of exams is to display one's abilities as opposed, for example, to answering the questions which one finds most interesting (in a related situation, I chose two of my three A-level subjects on the basis that they were subjects that I was interested by but not very good at and therefore it seemed more important to me to improve my abilities in these areas than to waste time on subjects that I was already good at). It is important to make these unspoken rules clear, and to teach exam skills such as reading questions carefully, allocating specific amounts of time to particular sections and switching between different topics.

We typically fail to take into account the possible implications of what we say and do on our social relationships with our classmates:

In the second or third grade, the class began discussing souls and God. Being raised in an atheist house, I had no idea about these concepts and proceeded to let the whole world know how stupid they were for keeping their 'imaginary friend.' This did not make me very popular, as I recall. (Charles)

My school reports usually contained comments such as:

While expressing her views with admirable vigour, Clare could occasionally make more allowance for the tentative opinions of others … (school report, 1990)

This last comment is a masterpiece of understatement, given that at the time (my teens) I believed that I was being extremely helpful in English lessons by explaining to my classmates why they were wrong, complete with meticulous point-by-point demolitions of their views. As I saw it, we were there in order to study the texts and analyse them in a logical way, and we were surely all united in our aim of establishing the truth. How could we learn or progress if people didn't point out mistakes or ambiguities? After my teacher told me that I was upsetting the others, I gradually came to realize that I was contravening some sort of social rule, and tried over the years to restrain myself, but still find it baffling and counter-intuitive. It wasn't until I was studying philosophy at university, where it was made clear that we should attempt to shred each others' arguments without restraint and that our tutors would do likewise to us (with the understanding that none of this was remotely personal but that this challenging was essential to learning and independent thought) that I finally felt at home.

Teaching which emphasizes the ability to work co-operatively in a group is liable to penalize the student with Asperger's. We are likely to be seen as "stand-offish" and un-co-operative:

> In a collaborative group [art] project which demanded a high level of cooperation Clare was not very communicative and somewhat taciturn … (school report, 1988)

More importantly, a student with Asperger's required to work as part of a group of neurotypical students is likely to find the experience both stressful and ineffective as a way of learning:

> There is a lot of group work in the public school system. I usually don't know how to participate in group work and am blamed for not participating. A lot of the group work assigns people to draw something on a piece of butcher paper. One assignment was to draw a metaphor of the United States government. The group decided to compare it to a beach. Four days were spent on this project. They were drawing a beach the whole time, not learning about the way the government works. The other students may have made references to the government a few times, but only a minority of the time. Although I can understand the purpose of this assignment, I feel that just teaching the references that the other students made would have only taken a few minutes. The other students may learn best through this method of teaching, but I don't.

Increased awareness of the rest of the class as an audience (sometimes as a result of being ridiculed in front of or by them) could lead to a sense of extreme vulnerability – Donna Williams' term "exposure anxiety" seems appropriate here. Being called on and required to speak or even read aloud in front of a class could be a cause for terror:

> [I was] always being afraid the enemy teacher would try to make me participate in the group. I would always go completely blank or mumble something unintelligible and they'd finally call on someone else. (Jack)

For some people, even being looked at by others or doing anything that might attract attention could be intensely stressful and overloading:

> I remember once I was late leaving the house, and it was 2 minutes before bell time by the time I was half way there, so there was no way I could

arrive on time. It was assembly too, so I would have had to enter assembly late, or else find some other occupation for 15 minutes. Entering assembly late would mean entering the room alone at the front and being the centre of attention for a moment, which I couldn't bear the thought of. So I just turned 180 degrees and walked back home! ... Another area where I had difficulty was leaving my seat (personal space), say if I had to go to the front of the room to give a sick note to the teacher, or even putting my hand up to ask for a new book. (David Hawker)

Learning and learning styles

Most pupils with Asperger's syndrome have a highly idiosyncratic learning style, and where school fails to accommodate this, we are unable to learn and may suffer agonies of boredom and frustration. Jack commented that:

... the boring subject matter and the teachers' styles, the whole set-up of school, prohibited me from being able to learn much of anything.

Sitting through hours and hours of lessons which are so inaccessible that they might as well be in another language can be a trauma in itself:

What was the most traumatic thing about school? The boredom. (Joseph)

Many people with Asperger's have a predominantly visual style of thinking and learning ("thinking in pictures" as Temple Grandin 1995, describes it) and benefit from teaching strategies that emphasize pictures and/or written text (some visually-oriented people with Asperger's, like me, also have hyperlexia, displaying unusually early and fast reading abilities – not always accompanied by equal levels of comprehension. Sarah remembered "from age 3 my favorite 'toy' was the dictionary and I would spend hours poring through its pages"):

At school and during my first degree I was helped by the fact that I could read up topics in advance, things were also written down on the blackboard, the work tended to follow a logical progression and because new material was being put across to students, teachers could not talk too fast, rather they seemed to leave gaps of a second or two between each sentence which enabled me to guess more accurately what I had heard. (Joliffe, 1992, p. 14)

As this suggests, a visual learning style is often accompanied by auditory processing problems:

As I grew up, I often had problems following conversations and would often blank out while trying to listen to what other people are saying. Very

*often in grade school (and on through high school), I would say 'Huh?' or
'What?' because I failed to hear what someone had said to me. This would
especially be the case if I had to selectively listen to one person in a room
full of chatter or noise. (Sarah)*

Carol reported that as a small child with significant language delays:

*If I did pay attention to what was being said, it was as if everyone was
talking to me even if they were talking to someone else or even if the talk
was coming from the TV. That got overwhelming at times. I was constantly
on edge and aggravated when I tried to focus on language and other
people talking. It was kind of like having ten radios blaring with each one
of them slightly off the station and trying to listen to each one of them.*

*On the other hand, when my mother would try shutting everything off and
try to get me to focus on her and what she was saying, that too was
overwhelming. I would hear her words, but they just didn't make any sense. I
felt like a deer caught in the headlights of an oncoming tractor trailer rig.*

Simply holding spoken information in short-term memory long enough
to make sense of it may be difficult, even though the same person, asked to repeat
what has been said, may be able to echo it back without comprehension. Even at
university, lectures were almost completely useless to me, as after only a few
minutes I would find that I could hold the beginning of a sentence in my mind, and
then the end, but not grasp the whole long enough to extract the meaning.

However, not all people with Asperger's share this learning style, and
some have exactly the reverse, finding auditory information far easier to process
than visual:

*… visual stimuli simply don't enter my brain in a meaningful way. This was
probably the reason why I used to talk to myself all the time. I translated
everything explicitly in language. Teachers should do the same. They should
talk children like me through every problem. Preferably, they should teach
children to do this for themselves. (Darius)*

The common denominator of autistic learning styles is concreteness:
we typically have great difficulty in moving from specific details to perceiving an
overall "gestalt" or pattern:

*We had to learn topography and I learned this at home with the map my
parents owned. The next week we had to take a test. The big school map
was hung in front of the class and the teacher would point to cities and
we'd have to write down the name. I failed abysmally. I now know why this
happened. The map at home had different colours. When I learned from
the map at home it was lying flat on the table. The map in school hung*

down from the ceiling and the background (table vs. wall) was also quite different. I still have the same problems. A street entered from the south is a different (and to me unfamiliar) street than the same street entered from the north. (Darius)

Comprehension and relevance

A concrete learning style combined with difficulties in social understanding can create problems of comprehension of texts, particularly when essential points are implied rather than directly stated, or must be deduced by connecting different pieces of information (it's as if bits of information go into separate files in my mind and it is not automatic for me to work out what implications one bit will have for another). The "weak central coherence" theory is particularly applicable here:

When I am reading a book I don't always understand what I am reading and it is so frustrating and I don't get how to summarize things and make generalisations. They describe irrelevant things and things I have no interest in and have no idea what to do with, like every detail on a log. (Quinn)

Determining what is and what is not relevant can be almost impossible, especially since the natural focus of our interest may in any case be very different from the "norm". When writing, we may end up accumulating vast amounts of information on what are deemed to be trivial points, while leaving out what seems, from the teacher's perspective, to be the whole point:

I sometimes had problems judging relevance and this is best shown in an essay I had to write in my sixth grade composition book on my trip to the Polynesian Cultural Center. My essay mentioned almost nothing about the events at the Center and focused almost entirely on irrelevant details of my journey to the Center and back: 'Yawn! I just got up. The time is 6:15. Today is the excursion to the Polynesian Cultural Center. I fix myself some Raisin Bran. Then I brush my teeth. Time is 7:50, time to go to school. We arrive at school and I quickly board the bus. Time is 9:00. We are about in Kaneohe. I'm probably talking to Kevin about clothes that won't burn or about 18 frogs. Time is 9:30. We arrive at the Polynesian Cultural Center. We have games, and many googie things. Time is 6:00 A.M. the next day. We have a terrific buffet breakfast. Time is 2:30. We arrive at our school. Our parents pick us up and we go home.' (Sarah)

Lack of awareness of what others can and cannot be expected to know often causes problems with "showing your working". I never understood why I had to do this: to me, the fact that I had put the correct answer to a maths question, for example, should be enough and I didn't see why I had to write out in detail (laboriously, given my appalling handwriting) how I had arrived at it, especially since the way of solving the problem that seemed intuitively clear to me was often not the prescribed method. In some cases, I didn't even have any working to put down; the answer was just obvious to me, and I couldn't work out what needed explaining. Similarly, in writing essays, I would often refuse to include particular points because they were so obvious. It had to be explained to me (repeatedly) that, no matter how stupid it seemed to me, I needed to show examiners that I did know this basic material before demonstrating more advanced knowledge.

Detailed feedback on work can help to overcome some problems of comprehension, but it needs to be positive and non-punitive – David A. commented that specific grades might have been helpful "if they hadn't been used to bash me with …"The most useful feedback not only indicated errors, but also clarified how things needed to be changed. David Hawker commented:

Marked past papers with comments were great.

In order to avoid problems of comprehension affecting the usefulness of feedback itself, it is important to have a framework within which criticism can be understood (I have never been able to judge, without being explicitly told, whether a criticism means that I am about to fail the course or whether it indicates the one problem that needs to be remedied before my work is completely perfect):

I always found it helpful if evaluators would organize their feedback, so as to help to distinguish which parts of their critique I should focus on and which are less important. It's very easy for me to get bogged down on the wrong details and then proceed to have a nervous breakdown. I like the concept of a 'knowledge framework' and appreciating help relating different concepts to each other so that feedback can be used to improve my understanding, which of course, improves my ability to perform. (Alice)

A note on computers

Children with Asperger's syndrome are sometimes described as thinking like computers or robots and indeed the concreteness and rigidity characteristic of our learning style often seems to have a natural affinity with the workings of computers. A disproportionate number of people with Asperger's syndrome work in the computer industry (which offers a helpful niche in the stereotype of the "computer geek") and some people have even suggested that Bill Gates displays some autistic traits. In the classroom, this affinity can be a powerful tool for learning, and provide an area of expertise for the child with Asperger's that may even be respected and admired by others. Learning in solitary communion with a computer is a natural and happy state for many people with Asperger's and many people emphasized the need to provide such opportunities for children with Asperger's:

> If a kid has problems concentrating or learning, see how he will do on a computer as compared to the usual classroom recitations and groups. Allow more for differences. (Jack)

Fred described his introduction to computers as literally life-saving:

> (My) teacher got me into early Apple II computers. Ironically, I was the last kid in the class to touch the thing - I was afraid and standing in the corner when all of the kids were playing around. Once he helped me overcome my fear, I quickly became the most knowledgeable in the class and was totally addicted. As a matter of fact, my self-esteem was boosted after being suicidal months before.

Routines and structure

Our concrete learning style seems to be connected to our intense need for routines and predictability. Neurotypical children are able to extract an overall picture of what is going on and can safely disregard "unimportant" details. For us, there is not such thing as an unimportant detail, and we may experience cause great distress if we cannot predict what will happen in our environment or make sense of the changes that do occur:

> School causes a lot of anxiety for me. There might be a new rule of event I would not be able to know how to handle. I can never understand the point of these rules (probably because there isn't one). I would be constantly paranoid and worried about what I would have to do, and had no clue what to do. Things like this caused me to not want to go to school. (Quinn)

Consequently, it is important to ensure that the day and the week have a predictable shape and order, and that any alteration or interruption of the schedule (for example, different events to mark the last day of term) are talked about and explained well in advance. If promises of any sort are made, then they must be honoured and when statements which cannot be guaranteed in this way, then this should be made clear by adding "probably" or "maybe". Not knowing what's happening or not being able to predict what's going to happen next, even when it comes to apparently "trivial" details, can generate great anxiety.

For those who learn visually, visual schedules such as those used in the TEACCH system can be extremely helpful, and teaching a child how to make their own schedules (and lists or checklists for things to be done) can be extremely helpful. For the whole of secondary school, I invented my own visual schedules on small pieces of paper that I could carry around in my pocket and refer to continually.

It is important to differentiate between "structured" and "directive" environments, as the two are often confused. Particularly when it comes to children with behavioural problems, references to a "structured" environment often indicate one which is tightly controlled, with strictly enforced rules. The "structure" needed by children with Asperger's syndrome, in contrast, refers to *order*, not control; in fact, it is important to share control and involve children in planning their schedule (for example, a child and their teacher could agree together that on Fridays the child will have an hour after lunch in which to work in the library on a project on their latest obsession). What matters is whether the order of events is predictable and legible (presented in a format that the child can grasp and hold in their mind), not who is in control.

Communication

Our distinctive learning styles can cause problems interpreting language and we are usually highly pedantic (demanding that the meaning of words be used precisely and rigidly) and very literal:

> *I also had a few problems with some of the idioms that people used; I tended to interpret them too literally. If someone asked me, 'Don't you want ice cream?' I would respond 'No' if I wanted some, because I thought they wanted to know if I didn't want ice cream. Or a question like 'You want some ice cream, don't you?' would confuse me since it seemed like it was posing two opposite questions at the same time, if I wanted ice cream and if I didn't want ice cream. I also had trouble understanding negative responses which were in agreement with a negative statement, i.e. 'You can't divide three evenly into seven.', 'No, you certainly can't.' I would absolutely require the response to be, 'Yes, you certainly can't.' But the one I hated the most was 'Do you mind if ...' I would always get mixed up if the person asking the question wanted to know if I minded what they were asking or if it was okay for them to do what they were asking. I often gave the opposite response than expected, so I learned to give elaborated responses like, 'Yes, it's okay if you did that.' It would particularly be difficult if the question was phrased as a negative, i.e. 'You don't mind if I do that, do you?' I would not know if I'm supposed to say 'Yes' or 'No' and I don't know what people conventionally say ... I also recall having trouble understanding the expression "shut up" when I was in fourth grade; since I knew the word "shut" only from 'shut the door,' I asked the person who told me to shut up, 'Do you mean shut the door and pull it up? (Sarah)*

This literalism can cause many problems with communication in the classroom, particularly when it comes to understanding rules and instructions.

Typically, we do not generalize from specific instances to overall principles (for example, not understanding that "don't play with fire" also forbids playing with stoves even if they do not have an open flame) – and if we do, we may overgeneralize (for example, deciding that all fiction is lying and therefore forbidden):

> I also strongly began to dislike fiction during this period. I somehow got the idea in my head that since fictional works do not describe actual events, writing fiction is tantamount to lying. This is typical of my overly literal approach to life. Another example is an occasion in fifth grade when I decided, for reasons unclear to me now, to place grapes on the stove until they bore grill markings and then place them in the freezer until they froze solid. My mom discovered the grapes in the freezer and confronted me with the evidence, asking me if I had done this. I said that I did and then she lectured me about 'playing with fire.' Immediately I balked at this, telling her that I did no such thing, realizing in my mind that there was no fire to be found on the electric stove. My persistent denial of this resulted in the most severe penalty … (Sarah)

Characteristically, we view the world in black and white, with little ability to register or tolerate ambiguity:

> An example of my strict adherence to rules can also be found in an essay I wrote for English class (summer school after sixth grade). Commenting on a short story on wartime morals, I wrote: "Early in the story, the soldier said that the officer said, 'We are not here to save dogs.' But the soldier replied, 'He's got every right to be saved as anyone.' Now the choice is clear. They were NOT here to save dogs. It's so obvious – the dog is the one to be shot. (Sarah)

Literalism can result in "inexplicable" refusals when faced with "impossible" instructions, or panic when faced with what appear to be threats ("You're so sweet, I could eat you up"). It can be the source of many apparently irrational fears, especially since we typically have no ability to estimate the actual size of a risk. After seeing a poster warning about rabies at the airport on the way back from holiday one year, I then tried every tactic I could think of to avoid leaving the country at all next year because I was so terrified of getting rabies. After learning about germs, I insisted that any tiny scratch or cut *had* to be doused in antiseptic (my mother says I spent several years smelling strongly of TCP).

Communication between home and school can be as much of a problem as communication in the classroom. Problems with "theory of mind" (recognizing that others may not share the same information) mean that it is important not to rely on the child with Asperger's as a conduit for information.

My mother recalls that often, when she dropped me off at primary school, I would turn to her in a panic and demand, for example, "Where's the frying pan?" This would invariably be the first she'd heard of it and it would take lengthy interrogation of me to establish that everyone in the class had been told to bring a frying pan in; it had never occurred to me that she needed to be told this in order to provide it. Other people had similar problems:

> One of the most recurrent problems throughout middle childhood was my constant failure to distinguish between my knowledge and that of others. Very often my parents would miss deadlines or appointments because I failed to tell them of these matters. For instance, my parents missed the school's Open House in my fifth grade and my mom asked me afterward, 'Why didn't you tell us about it?' 'I thought you knew it,' I replied. 'I didn't know.' 'I knew it, I thought you knew it.' 'Well, I wouldn't know it unless you told me,' she said. This matter would come up time and time again, and we would always have the same argument. Sometimes I went to a neighbour's house and failed to tell her where I was, because I thought she knew. 'You have to tell me,' my mom would say, 'we have to communicate.' (Sarah)

Even people who were remarkably fluent verbally often had difficulty in spontaneously generating language in certain circumstances – for example, to ask for help or say that they didn't understand. David Hawker described one exam experience:

> It was an A-level physics paper that got me a U (so low it wasn't graded, like < 20%). I think the reason I scored so low was I didn't have my calculator with me to work out all the maths properly. I'd left it in my bag which I left outside the exam hall. When I realised I didn't have it, when the teacher asked if there were any problems, I was just plain too scared to put my hand up and communicate it. Partly because of fear of stammering when saying the word 'calculator' and partly out of being very reserved and unassertive and not liking to create a fuss. So I just struggled through the paper without the calculator...

Memory and attention

Attention is a key element in learning of any sort and, like so much else, it appears to function very differently from the "norm" in people with Asperger's syndrome. Many children with Asperger's syndrome experience painful difficulties in paying attention to lessons:

School takes up a large portion of the day. I don't have the attention span to pay attention the entire day. I think with the ways I would learn best, it would only take a smaller portion of the time. (Quinn)

However, it is important to be clear about the nature of these attention problems. Although many people experience both (sometimes qualifying for a dual diagnosis), Asperger's syndrome seems to produce attention problems of its own which are distinct from the short attention span and difficulty focusing characteristic of attention-deficit disorder, even though they may co-exist. Darius drew on Hans Asperger's brilliant distinction between distraction from without and distraction from within (Asperger, 1991, p. 75–6) in describing his school experiences:

Teachers … thought I was easily distracted. They were right, but it was not the type of attention problem most children have, which is that they can't focus and have a short attention-span. People like me are – as Asperger himself noticed – distracted from within. We have a very interesting inner thoughtscape and can daydream for ages. My associative thought processes lead me to ideas and possibilities much more interesting than the subjects taught in school.

I experienced a huge surge of relief when I read about Eric Courchesne's research on cerebellar abnormalities in autism which suggests that the cerebellum is involved in voluntary shifts of attention (see McDonnell 1993 p. 297, Grandin 1995 p. 68). I have never been able to control what I attend to, or pay attention to something on command, but had never had an explanation for this other than "daydreaming", "absent-mindedness" and so on. Problems with attention are all too often seen as wilfulness or laziness and my school reports regularly criticized me for "refusing" to pay attention to subjects which did not interest me:

… it is disappointing that she is unwilling to employ her talents in any area which momentarily does not interest her … she must not allow likes and dislikes to hinder her progress … (extracted from school reports, 1986–8)

Nobody believed I could have problems paying attention, given the complete absorption with which I could focus on some things. But I could not shift my attention from one subject to another by an act of will; it seemed to take a sort of mental "wrench" to manage it at all and the level of effort required meant I could only sustain it for short amounts of time before I switched off and was unable to take in any more information. On the basis of discussions with other people with Asperger's, this seems to be very typical. Being required to shift attention from one subject to another at half-hour intervals made things even worse. David A. commented that "changing attention-focus at THEIR pace was hard" and Jim reported that he was only able to switch attention between different subjects because "after second grade I was usually in schools where we would change classrooms for different subjects. This let me mentally shift gears."

This "stickiness" of attention can also make students vulnerable to distractions from without, particularly sensory ones: while a neurotypical person may be able to "tune out" a background stimulus like the hum of a heater or the flicker of fluorescent lights with ease, a student with Asperger's may, noticing it, find that their mind latches onto it and makes it impossible for them to switch their attention to the lesson being taught. It is particularly important to remove distracting background stimuli from the classroom since the student with Asperger's will not be able to filter them out.

Problems with attention may also be connected with the common problems that children with Asperger's have with rote memorization (learning times tables, for example). This is often particularly baffling and frustrating to teachers given that our memories are often excellent, in some cases eidetic, especially when it comes to accumulating facts on a topic that we are obsessed with.

Spontaneous accessing of memories of events could also be a problem, often in contrast to excellent memories for impersonal facts (see Jordan and Powell, 1995, pp. 6–8). When I had just started at school, every Monday we had to write out or dictate some sentences to copy about what we had done at the weekend. I remember that my mind always went blank when I tried to remember; I couldn't think of anything I had done at the weekend, although I know that if someone had prompted me with specific questions such as "Did you go to the park or to the swimming pool? What did you do at the park?" I would been able to answer accurately. I just couldn't access my memories on demand and I was terrified and frustrated at not being able to do what the teachers were telling me to do. Although I was very verbal, I didn't have the communicative skills to spontaneously say that I couldn't remember, so I made up stories instead (I didn't have any sense of what was plausible, though, so I was eventually found out).

Planning and organization

Closely connected to problems with attention are problems with executive planning, and children with Asperger's often end up perseverating, obsessively repeating a particular response even when it is no longer of use (repeating a question once it has been answered, for example, or repeating a strategy that has already failed to solve a problem). We are often unable to shift our attention away from the point at which we have become stuck, or generate new strategies to try. Conversely, we may pursue a single train of thought that we are interested in, unaware that it is leading us further and further away from the topic we are supposed to be concentrating on. These traits can cause significant problems when it comes to structuring work:

> I ... was bad at all subjects where one needed to structure oneself. I could always think of another interesting topic to write about in my papers, so they became sort of rambling ... (Darius)

Organizational abilities (being able to bring the right books to a lesson, for example) were also often affected. At secondary school, I adopted the strategy of carrying everything I might conceivably need at any point in the week around in my schoolbag at all times, out of fear that I might be caught without something I needed. Obviously, this strategy had a significant cost (the schoolbag got very, very heavy); nonetheless, it was the only way I was able to ensure that I arrived at my lessons with everything I needed.

Planning difficulties should not be confused with laziness; many people combined "absent-mindedness" and disorganization with extreme perfectionism. Often we end up getting "stuck" and perseverating about one detail or preliminary point and unable to get an overview of the project as a whole. Failing to estimate how long a piece of work will take, we may leave it until the night before the deadline, or end up spending all our free time on it because we feel it must be perfect and are unable to tell when it is "good enough" to count as finished. People reported:

> Because of my absent-mindedness and a tendency to be overwhelmed by details, I had problems with organization. I would not complete my schoolwork in an orderly fashion and sometimes took too long to finish something if I made an effort to be careful. (Sarah)

> I ... don't know how to start homework and get motivated to do it or finish it ... (Quinn)

Fred described:

> ... sniffing pencils, having my papers just so, but never really getting any assignments done on time ...

How to plan one's work, organize oneself and problem-solve (e.g. how to outline an essay, how to make a list of things to do, how to brain-storm possible solutions to a problem) need to be taught explicitly from early on.

Doing it by ourselves

Unable to learn from the teaching on offer, some children with Asperger's simply taught themselves, retreating to the library, a corner or even under a table or desk, which creates a private, safe-feeling space:

During this period, I began to spend more and more time in the library, which I regarded as a sanctuary. I would read from various picture books … science books and journals such as Science News. (Sarah)

What helped me learn a little was the fact that I was fond of reading and that I was able to use the library. Nothing else helped. (Jack)

All through elementary school and junior high, I was far enough ahead academically that the teachers let me do what I wanted, which was mostly just reading in the library or under a table. (Michelle)

They let me sit on the floor in the corner and teach myself calculus with crayons and upon request provided me with math and history books. After being bitten a few times they also figured out not to touch me. (Helen)

This autodidacticism could cause great frustration when teachers only acknowledged learning that took place in the classroom under their direction and refused to recognize what the child had taught themselves (when I was six, one of my teachers insisted that I had to proceed through the desperately boring books of the official reading scheme, despite the fact that in my spare time at school I was reading Gerald Durrell's *My Family and Other Animals*; I think, although my memory is not wholly clear, that I may even have been made to read the official reading scheme twice because I finished it so far in advance of the others):

Something else that really frustrates me is that I am in a math class and I am learning things that I have already figured out seven years ago. I am interested in other topics, but can't learn them because the pace is so incredibly slow. I also find it quite insulting … I personally think I could have learned a lot more at a faster pace. I have been figuring out things before they are taught as explained in the math section. I often try to figure out things by myself that I am interested in long before the school gets to the topics … When I learn something on my own, I tend to learn much more. I wonder what would it would be like if I were taught appropriately all my life (or at least since I started asking to be taught differently). I don't know why people would do this to me. My childhood has been wasted. (Quinn)

I have little question that I probably should have been accelerated from a very early age. I was often 1 to 2 years ahead in terms of 'age equivalency' at school for much of the early years and I really got bogged down in sheer and utter boredom. I attribute many of my difficulties now to not being allowed to proceed when I was ready and able, the waiting often rendering me anxious and burned out, never being able to capitalize on my natural enthusiasm (which I had no shortage of when I was younger). (Alice)

Often, we ended up with a very different view of the ideal role of teachers and schools in learning. Helen, explaining the problems caused by a move to a new school, wrote:

My old school let me determine what I needed and what I wanted and then provided resources. The new school told me how they planned to fix me and what was wrong … It is the child's life and they must determine its course. Teachers are resources.

When asked what would have helped him learn, David A. replied: "the chance to do my own learning with help from someone else, rather than to have them try to force me to learn things ..."

Motivation and obsessions

Motivating children with Asperger's syndrome is a major challenge for any teacher. Gunilla Gerland's (1997) comments suggest similarities to the problems of attention which I have already described:

I find it really hard to motivate myself to do things which don't come out of a genuine interest (if they do — then there's no limit of my motivation and effort). I found this very hard in school, and when I meet teachers today I see that some of them think their student is just 'un-motivated' or 'lazy' etc. I think there's something profoundly different about how my motivation works and that I should not be made culpable for this. Other, normally developed children, seem to have a lot of social motivation, like 'I want to do this because other kids are doing it', or 'look at what I just did', or 'I want to do this so that the teacher will like me better' etc. I have no access to this kind of motivation and I think it's important that the teacher really understands this. When I have to try and stretch out my personal motivation to embrace things which I don't find genuinely interesting, then this is a giant effort and sometimes I just fail to do it. (personal communication)

We have a fundamental inability to understand why we should do things which we find boring, pointless or stupid, let alone understanding why it is not even permissible to announce loudly as a statement of fact that particular work is "stupid" or "boring" (even saying that one would much rather do something else is often frowned on – I have a great deal of sympathy with one of Asperger's subjects, who "…when asked to work out 5 plus 6 … said 'I don't like little sums, I'd much rather do a thousand times a thousand.'" (Asperger, p. 75).

However, we can be incredibly strongly motivated to pursue an obsession, and this can result in extraordinary levels of work and learning. Sarah's account may give something of an idea of the level of intellectual drive involved in obsessions:

In fourth grade, I was … interested in both dinosaurs and Astronomy, especially since this was the time of the Voyager flybys of Jupiter and Saturn. My appetite for information was voracious and I would clip or photocopy everything I could find on the subject in the newspaper, magazines, academic journals and books. I think my interest in dinosaurs waned at this point, though I remember an occasion when I went to the neighbourhood pool and I went up to total strangers asking them to ask me any question about dinosaurs, because I felt I knew everything about them.

In fifth grade, I was still very much interested in astronomy … but my obsession du jour in fifth grade was weather, and I would study the newspaper every day and keep track of changes in temperature across the nation. In sixth grade, my interest in weather waned (partly because I was frightened of pictures of stormy weather) and I became interested in American Indians. I also was hugely interested in a soap opera my mom and I watched and I wrote down the story of the previous year into a running narrative.

That summer I attended summer school and reflected on my all-consuming interests in an essay for English class. In an essay on loneliness, I described my interests as a surrogate 'friend.' I wrote: 'Learning has no end. Brightness is a companion - one that can't go away. Curiosity can get you in troble [sic], but the troble is the best thing to happen - it will climax your work. When I was in third grade, I worked on a project, with a friend. Later on I could not work with her and my curiosity went loose. I studied A to Z on Cosmology, Insects, Whales, Dinosaurs, Dr. Einstein, Coins, Photography, American Indians, etc. Curiosity has no end ...'

In seventh grade, I became obsessed with tennis and wanted to devise a system of ranking the players of Wimbledon by the number of games won and lost. I perfected this system in tenth grade. But I also became interested in Egypt and Mesopotamia and started to study ancient history at length.

Then in eighth grade, my attention turned to the Bible and I was totally obsessed with the first twelve chapters of Genesis and began to write my own book about it. In particular, I was fascinated by the "so-and-so begat so-and-so" lists in Genesis and wanted to study the Hebrew etymologies of these names. Then I extended this interest with a growing interest in chronology, so that I wanted to harmonize the secular chronology of Mesopotamia with the biblical chronology of the period between the Flood and the birth of Abraham. I worked on this into my freshman year of high school but gave up.

By my sophomore year of high school, I became fascinated by Vikings (partly because of my Norwegian roots) and wanted to write my own novel. I sketched out a very complicated storyline that spanned three centuries. … I also became fascinated by the comparative method in historical linguistics which is how protolanguages are reconstructed. By the senior year of high school, I had compiled an enormous set of cognate lists of words from all the Indo-European and Austronesian languages. I would spend every lunch recess in the library studying the word etymologies in the dictionary. My friends thought I was such an über-nerd to be so fascinated by the dictionary and one day one of them stole one of my manila folders which were stuffed with notes and cognate lists.

All too often, obsessions are seen as pathological symptoms, which interfere with whatever the teacher is trying to teach and so need to be suppressed. I feel that this is an extraordinary waste of motivation and energy, particularly given how hard it can be to motivate children with Asperger's in other respects. Autistic author Temple Grandin has emphasized how important it is to channel and make use of obsessions to motivate learning; describing her "most important mentor in high school", she explains "The other teachers and professionals at the school wanted to discourage my weird interests and make me more normal, but Mr. Carlock took my interests and used them as motivators for doing schoolwork." (Grandin, 1995, p. 99). This is true no matter how bizarre an obsession may appear to others: Grandin's obsession with cattle-chutes became the inspiration for her PhD in animal science and successful career as one of the world experts in livestock handling design (she has designed one third of the livestock handling facilities in the United States). Sometimes it will be necessary to place a limit on an obsession (for example, by explaining to a child that talking about the Wars of the Roses in a maths lesson is not permitted), but distinguishing between permissible and impermissible outlets for an obsession is very different from suppressing or ignoring it altogether.

Asperger commented with his customary lucidity and insight that: "…there is an inability to learn from adults in conventional ways. Instead, the autistic individual needs to create everything out of his own thought and experience … He took away from the lesson only those things for which he had a particular affinity and could think about in his own way." (Asperger, p. 56)

In order for children with Asperger's to gain anything from lessons at all it is vital for teachers to recognize what we have an affinity for and present information in such a manner that we can "think about it in our own way."

5
In the Playground: the social environment

*School was a torture ground in itself for me because of my lack of social
skills and my absolute terror of people (in part because I didn't just
automatically know the social rules, and, when I did learn them, I had to
think about them all the time – and who can keep up that sort of coping
skill ALL THE TIME). (Karen)*

A recurrent, spontaneous image in many people's stories was that of being the
child in the corner or on the edge of the playground:

*I spent my recesses alone. I recall standing by myself on the edges of the
blacktop, watching the other kids inside play jump rope and basketball
while I tasted from the honeysuckle bushes on the sidelines. I did not yet
have a friend, though I did not particularly desire one either. (Sarah)*

*The thing that was the best during school hours was when I went way out
in a field with my miniature people and cars and played in the sand or on
a log by myself. (Jack)*

This was often the only partial escape from the sea of noise, people
and flying balls (Fred wrote:"My first memorable experience with a ball on recess
was this damn kickball coming out of nowhere and slamming me in the head" –
as I know from personal experience, this apparently trivial event could be
shocking and traumatic) and the only place where one could think about a
favourite obsession and hope not to be disturbed.

At primary school, when my class was taken to a local park, I used to
sit in the flowerbeds and eat weeds. It was only years later that I realized how
odd this was. At the time it was perfectly logical: I liked sitting behind the bushes
so I could be on my own and no-one could see me and I liked eating the weeds
because there was a certain sort that tasted very nice.

In such a refuge, children could observe others from a safe distance, or
escape into private worlds of thought. Some constructed elaborate "paracosms"

private worlds, which might be acted out with miniature figures or written down or kept safely internal (often these formed the seed of a lifelong interest in science fiction and fantasy books). I discovered that if I found a patch of grass, I could move into it mentally, "zooming in" on its tiny details and imagining it to be a forest.

Even when children were older and breaks were spent inside, they could be equally frightening and hard to cope with: "Socialising, hanging around to get involved in stuff, help teachers with things, etc., seemed terrifying …" (David Hawker). Early experiences on the playground seemed to set the tone for all social experiences throughout school.

Interactions with other children: bullying, teasing and isolation

Bullying and teasing were almost invariably part of the school experience of children with Asperger's, with many people reporting being "teased constantly":

They called me the 'sixth form punch bag' as I was probably about the only kid who got bullied in 6th form (A-levels). (David Hawker)

I was put in with a lot of dumb bullies who constantly taunted me … [the teacher] always blamed me for pranks such as putting chalk in the eraser, when it was the other kids who did that and always relished the blame that I got. (Fred)

Jean-Paul recalled "… being cornered in the hall, shower, bathroom, being taunted, teased, physically and verbally threatened and publicly humiliated by the bullies."

I was comparatively lucky in that I was rarely hit (I was jostled and shoved, and had my pants pulled down in gym, but mostly, I was just teased). In many cases bullying included physical violence, sometimes extreme, and sexual violence featured in at least one case:

8th grade boys would bully me and on occasion knocked me off my bike on the way home from school. The result that day was a bleeding lip and a chipped front tooth, which was later repaired by a dentist. To this day, I can tell where the chipped part was when I look in the mirror. (Karen)

I got hanged [with wire around the neck] and other kinds of what the staff called mild teasing … Someone ejaculated over my trousers in front of the whole class … no-one helped me … Things for me were somewhat more than the teasing issues … it was torture and abuse. (David A.)

In many respects, children with Asperger's make "perfect victims", a fact that most bullies are quick to discover: we have no tactics for verbal or physical self-defense, we are extraordinarily naïve, we almost never tell and we can be reduced to tears of frustration and rage with delicious ease by simple ploys like making fun of our obsessions. David Hawker explained:

I always found it difficult or awkward to get up and stand up for myself – raising my voice, rising to a conflict, telling someone off. Being assertive and tough. Thus, I was bullied a lot because of being odd or different and they knew they could do it to me without me fighting back or reporting it to a member of staff.

Often, "normal" peers discovered that they could terrify a child with Asperger's without having to lay a finger on them, by exploiting their gullibility and literal-mindedness:

I can remember some children chasing me home from kindergarten, telling me that since I liked animals so much they were going to cut me up into bacon. They described the whole process, telling me what they were going to do and how they were going to do it. I didn't eat bacon for about three years, I thought it was made from little kids no one liked.

That was almost 30 years ago. Would you like to know the names of the children? What they were wearing that day? About six years ago, I supervised one of them at work. He didn't even remember – he said it was just 'kid stuff' and meant nothing. I still don't understand that. (Jim)

It did not even occur to many people, myself included, to tell parents what was happening. I just didn't think of it, which is not surprising given that at that time I hadn't really worked out that I needed to tell people things in order for them to know them. In some ways I think I just assumed that school was supposed to be like that (my mother remembers that I would refuse to go into the school buildings in the morning and would run round and round her in little circles, but I was never able to tell her why I didn't want to go).

It requires a certain level of social competence even to categorize what is happening as "bullying". I mainly remember a painful confusion, not really knowing whether what was happening was accidental or intentional, whether this was supposed to be happening or not. Other children were baffling and frightening almost all the time; it's only now, looking back, that I can classify some of that as "bullying".

Bullies themselves may sometimes claim "it was an accident" or "I was just joking" and it may be almost impossible for a child with Asperger's to judge whether such statements are likely to be true or not.

Often children were left very unclear about whether the bullying was their fault, especially if they were blamed for it, or if bullying came from teachers themselves:

> As my teachers meted out such punishments, they would threaten to tell my parents how 'bad' I was, so I never told my parents anything for fear they would think I was bad. (Charles)

All too often, teachers responded to bullying of pupils with Asperger's either by "turning a blind eye" to it or actually condoning it:

> ... the severe beatings and abuse that I was taking from the other children were pointedly ignored by the school staff. They turned 'a blind eye.' (Schuyler)

> I was badly bullied and again teachers insulted me and said it was my fault for behaving like a prat. (Simon)

> They were absolutely aware, but did nothing ... if I tried [to tell them about it], I was told not to be childish. I was still a f***ing child, for Christ's sake! (David A.)

Many teachers seemed to concur with the bullies that children with Asperger's were "asking" to be bullied by behaving in odd and unlikeable ways or that it would somehow teach them to behave more "normally". "Mild" bullying was often seen as a normal part of the "rough and tumble" of childhood, and a child who reacted in a way seen as disproportionate, by bursting into tears, might be seen as "over-reacting", "attention-seeking" or a "cry-baby".

I will explore later the possible reasons why teachers themselves may sometimes be prone to "misread" children with Asperger's and to react instinctively in unhelpful and punitive ways; in the meantime, I have to note that, in a frightening number of cases, teachers themselves acted as bullies, often insulting and ridiculing children with Asperger's (usually in front of the class) or singling them out for punishment:

> ... many teachers actively made fun of me rather than showing sympathy ... One of my teachers called me a 'dickhead' in class for neglecting most of my school equipment one lesson. (Simon)

> I have many memories of primary school but none of them are pleasant. I remember being dragged by my fourth grade teacher down to the 4m x 3m infirmary room, where I was locked for six hours each day for a week. Since there was an adjoining bathroom, I had no 'need' to leave, and the door was locked anyway ... I was constantly ridiculed in front of my classmates. (Charles)

When asked, "What would you like teachers of kids with Asperger's to know?", David A. simply replied "That they have the capacity to damage a kid for life …"

"Traditional" forms of teasing and bullying, such as hoaxes on April Fool's Day, sticking "kick me" signs on people's backs, or the ritual chant of "a pinch and a punch, first of the month" (I was pinched – hard – and punched on the first of each month, barring school holidays, for several years), are often not classed by teachers as bullying at all, or are treated as jokes, with the victim being treated as a "bad sport" if they react with humiliation, fear and pain, instead of "seeing the funny side" (lest anyone doubt the sophistication, complexity, and brutality of children's culture, a list of chapter subheadings covering different traditions in *The Lore and Language of Schoolchildren* by Iona and Peter Opie (1959) includes "Sending Away. Inducing Quiet. Intimidation. Fighting. Retribution. Ordeals. Tortures. Hair Pulling").

I used to spend each April Fool's Day in a constant state of nervous anticipation (Jim recalled: "I used to skip school on April Fool's day …").

When teachers did address bullying, they often did so by advising the child with Asperger's on how to act ("act more confidently" "just ignore them") rather than directly intervening. Putting the onus on the victim to end the bullying in this way is usually ineffective, particularly since children with Asperger's can only obey such instructions in a literal way and typically do not have the social skills to use them flexibly as defences.

As well as bullying, all children with Asperger's experienced pervasive isolation, both voluntary and involuntary. Some avoided social interaction from fear and incomprehension (or simple lack of interest); those who did want to make friends were usually rejected:

> *I avoided and feared [classmates]. I was too immature for those my own age for one thing. I did not understand other kids or why they did the things they did. I wanted to be as far from them as possible.*

> *They mainly ignored me. Sometimes they made fun of me but I did my best to tune them out. I used to like to swing in playground swings for hours. If I thought kids were around that looked threatening, I would leave. I was fortunate in that I looked younger than my age so I could swing all I wanted even when I was a teenager and nobody paid attention to me, at least on the public playground. I wanted to be socially isolated. The only time I was not socially isolated is when the teachers forced me to play sports or join a class group. (Jack)*

> *I could not learn the rules to the games that other children played and I would mostly spend my time by myself. I would also not know how to defend myself and I suffered quite a bit of abuse at the hands of other*

kids. Most people thought I was "weird" and by the time I got into high school, the 'nerd' label attached itself pretty well ... I did begin to desire friends and I finally had a genuine friend in 3rd and 4th grades, but by 5th grade nobody wanted to really associate with me. (Sarah)

When I got to secondary school, I wasn't actively bullied anymore; I was just continually aware that no-one liked me, that whenever we were told to pair up in lessons, for example, I was always the one left over. Even if there were even numbers in the class, the teacher would still have to order someone else to form a pair with me. It wasn't until I was about 16 that I made any friends at all and even then I couldn't name someone whose "best friend" I was. I could only conclude that I was basically unlikeable.

The teens could be excruciatingly painful for students with Asperger's, as we watched all our classmates find boyfriends/girlfriends, go to parties and so on, and understood that our abysmal failure to do any of these (whether or not we actually would have wanted to, had we had the choice) damned us as "sad" and "losers".

Why?

Other schoolchildren seem to have a very limited tolerance for social deviance of any sort, however subtle, and for children with Asperger's, the complex system of "abstract symbols in perpetual motion" (Jerome Bruner's description of social behaviour, quoted in Peeters and Gillberg, 1999, p. 111) is impossible to decipher or operate with any degree of fluency:

I ... had trouble learning the rules to the games the other children played and I often played the wrong way, causing the other kids to avoid me as well or tease me ... My reactions to various situations were not quite what people expected. A kid would, for instance, greet me with smiles but I would sometimes give no response, which gave others the impression that I was unfriendly. I knew that I did not act right but I often was at a loss to know what I was doing wrong. Some of the things I did struck others as very strange. At the time I was really interested in dinosaurs and I occasionally used dinosaur names to express the relative size of objects, such as, 'That is a really brontosaurus car.' ... I made some new friends on a trip ... in fourth grade but I lost them only hours later by irritating them while they tried to sleep. This event contributed greatly to my reputation as a 'weirdo,' since the method I used to keep them awake was by making noises and talking to myself... As far as social interaction is concerned, it would not occur to me naturally to do something (or not do something) out of kindness, respect, or appreciation of someone. Social rules like saying please and thank you, reciprocating someone else's kind act and so forth, would be beyond me. I would need to be reminded to do one thing or another, or it would occur to me afterwards, usually when it's too late ... There was another student whom I thought resembled a cat, so I 'meowed' whenever she spoke to me, which she thought was strange ... (Sarah)

People probably assume I am stuck up and rude because of inappropriate social responses. For example I did not know I was supposed to say hi to people when they said hi to me until I was 13, and I wasn't able to make it a habit until age 14. It's still difficult to understand some things. Like if someone gives you something (like someone who passes out a piece of paper) it is appropriate to say thank you. I have trouble determining exactly which situations to say thank you in, or how to say it, or reacting fast enough. (Quinn)

Karen remembered "staying on one subject too long, not really following a conversation well, being scared to death of the phone, because there was no body language or facial expression that I could even try to go by in a phone conversation, etc. ..."

Charles remembered "I had this uncanny habit of saying or doing the worst possible thing at the worst possible time ..."

Some social rules could be learnt by rote, but without fluency or the ability to improvise around them in socially acceptable ways:

One thing that's always puzzled me is that there are people who can break the social rules without any penalty. I must say that it has annoyed me at times when I feel like I've taken the considerable time and effort to learn the rules and then others can break them at will ... (Elizabeth)

Some people copied certain behaviours "wholesale" from others, mimicking one person's sarcastic tone or another's idioms. In a few cases, people would actually adopt entire personas (this process seems to be described in some of Donna Williams' books). Often, an impression of social competence can be given with a collection of such tricks, rather as computer programs like ELIZA can sometimes pass for human on the basis of equally crude strategies (at secondary school, I developed a routine of echoing back any greetings I received – this worked well until someone said "Happy Birthday" to me). However, the fact that this technique can create a façade of normality does not mean that the person understands all their implications or is able to use them to communicate what they want or need.

Often, children with Asperger's fail to shift strategies in different situations and many of us have an ultra-formal manner, with a highly elaborate and pedantic vocabulary (a common cause of ridicule) and extreme difficulty in adopting a "casual" and "informal" manner (I signed letters to close relatives "Yours sincerely, Clare Sainsbury", until I was 18 or so). Equally, we may have trouble understanding that it is not okay to swear or say "crap" in front of a teacher.

It has sometimes been stated that people with Asperger's lack a sense of humour, but I think that this is subtly inaccurate: it is not a sense of humour we lack, but rather the social skills to recognize when others are joking, signal that we ourselves are joking, or appreciate jokes which rely on an understanding of social conventions. Perception of incongruity and a sense of proportion seem to be key elements in much humour and both are areas where people with Asperger's may perceive things very differently from the norm. Typically, we will make jokes which other people don't understand (or at "inappropriate" times or places), while failing to recognize the jokes or sarcasm of others:

> My attempts at humour during this period are … fairly obscure and one example has a note from my teacher indicating that she couldn't follow my humour. One example is a cartoon of a man trying to sell a boxed product on television and I had to fill in the quotation bubbles with humorous text. I labelled the box with the fairly opaque name 'Juck boxk' and the last cell, depicting the product pitcher holding the box while standing in the shower, was written with the following incomprehensible dialogue: 'Wow! You can be so hungry, o yum! It can be rock if you are in the showe [sic]! You can eat it in 5 sec.' (Sarah)

Consequently, we are handicapped when it comes to using humour as a social tool. For example, having read about jokes "defusing" situations, I once attempted to soothe a classmate who was angry with me by making a joke about how short she was. I quickly realized that this strategy had been a big mistake, but it took me a long time to work out why.

Commonly we have great difficulty tolerating being laughed at, even in a "friendly" way, and can become very upset by jokes about things which we take seriously. While this is partly due to social problems and cognitive inflexibility, it is also important to recognize that it is not any more acceptable to make fun of the eccentricities or obsessions of a child with Asperger's than it would be to make fun of the involuntary movements of a child with cerebral palsy. It is not defensible to claim to be "laughing with" (instead of "at") someone, as neurotypical people so often do, if *they* aren't laughing.

Often, lack of social skills, combined with clumsy movements and a voice which was often monotonous or odd in intonation, created what other schoolchildren saw as a "mental" or "spastic" manner:

> Other students don't think very highly of me at school. A lot of people just look at me and assume that I am not very smart. They think I am rude and stuck up. They assume they know everything about me. For a long

*time I did not know what people thought about me. I never knew what
terrible things people said about me for a long time. I don't know exactly
why people assume low intelligence. It probably has to do with the way I
walk or talk. It is probably also due to the fact that I don't socialize much
and don't talk much. (Quinn)*

In fact, while I was of primary school age, people who met me outside
school situations (the dentist, for example) and who didn't engage me in
intellectual conversation would sometimes *assume* that I had learning difficulties –
in fact, the dentist only found out I didn't when he started explaining to my mum
that this sort of jaw problem was of course very common in kids who were
"mentally handicapped".

Lack of social awareness could result in choosing clothes which were
deemed unfashionable and the development of basic hygiene and grooming skills
could also be delayed:

*Having fashion sense, keeping up with hygiene and socializing in larger
groups of people were skills that only began to solidify for me in my years
after graduating from high school. (Karen)*

*By my last year in high school I started making a bit more effort to fit in
(I actually started combing my hair every day, for instance). (Joseph)*

Sensory anomalies may mean that a child clings to a favourite garment
that has a tolerable texture or a familiar smell and refuses to allow it to be put to
the wash when it's dirty or thrown away when it actually starts to fall apart
(one partial solution, which I have adopted, is to buy many identical copies of any
favourite garment).

Many people with Asperger's syndrome fail to adopt the behaviour
which society deems appropriately "masculine" or "feminine". This can be a strength
in many respects – we are largely immune to gender stereotyping and do not
limit ourselves on the basis of what is deemed proper for girls or boys – but it
can also be yet another cause for bullying and isolation.

Some people with Asperger's syndrome are additionally handicapped
by a greater or lesser degree of prosopagnosia (a highly specific neurologically-
based difficulty in recognizing faces):

*"I only recognise people if I see them in the same context and if they
wear the same type of clothes. It takes many years before I learn to
recognise people in more than one situations or with different clothes.
Even then, meeting them in an unexpected situation/place will result in
blank stares from me because I don't recognise them …" (Darius)*

After five years at my primary school, I still couldn't recognize or name many of my classmates. At the end of secondary school, I still couldn't distinguish classmates who had the same colour hair and same haircut. Obviously, all of these factors exacerbate our social handicaps.

With hindsight, some people realized that other children had occasionally made overtures to them, which they had not recognized or responded to at the time:

> Now I kick myself when I look back and saw some people making the effort to reach out, but I was blind to them and let those possible friendships slip away. During that year, I sat at the nerd table in the cafeteria, jamming food down the heater and never really making any close friends. (Fred)

One of my few friends from secondary schools reported that she thought some other people had wanted to get to know me, but hadn't known how. At the time, I had been completely unaware of this; if anything, some things that may have been intended as friendly gestures left me baffled and vaguely frightened.

Conversely, when children with Asperger's did try to "make friends", with no idea of how to do so, we often ended up following someone around, hanging around them, asking "Will you be my friend?", and being rejected as annoying. Joseph explained:

> Wishing to join a conversation or a group activity ... [people with Asperger's] will be completely unaware of the subtle ways of initiating contact 'appropriately', and will instead either blunder in an interrupting way, or hover around on the fringes of the group without awareness that their presence is seen as either ridiculous or creepy and even threatening.

My rare attempts to play with others as a small child usually consisted of developing an elaborate game or story with arcane rules which nobody fully understood except me and demanding that others act out parts in the story in accordance with my instructions.

Often the people who were willing to make friends with us did so chiefly out of pity and a self-conscious desire to be kind to a poor unfortunate. Karen reflected that her only friend at one point had been: "a friend because of pity/compassion not an equal give and take friendship, I think". The outcome of such kindness could be closer to being made a "pet" of, or a teacher-student relationship, than a genuine companionship.

If and when children with Asperger's did make real friends, it was usually with "nerds", social rebels or other unconventional children:

> I had a few friends who were, for want of a better term, nerds of the library, computer and Star Trek varieties ... I couldn't care less whether I

was "popular" or not and didn't understand what the big deal was about. I spent all my lunch recesses in the library, either reading or spending time with my 'nerdish' friends. (Sarah)

... there were so many other introverted nerds there that I felt more at home. (Michelle)

Paradoxically, the obliviousness to social codes and inability to fit in of a student with Asperger's could sometimes lead to their being perceived as intentionally rebellious and therefore cool, occasionally providing a social niche:

... my quirky ways, obnoxious individualism and torn jeans made me very popular amongst the brand new Nirvana crowd. (Charles)

It is worth noting that those few children willing to go against the group verdict by becoming friends with a child with Asperger's are often remarkable individuals themselves, possessed of unusual courage and thoughtfulness. In some cases a child's obsessions could become the basis of a friendship and there is clearly a possible role for teachers in "matching" children with similar interests. Darius suggested "I was passionate about history and archaeology, so if there had been a club I could have joined, I could talk with other kids about interests we shared without looking too weird."

The effects of bullying and isolation

The psychological effects of bullying and isolation were often devastating and could be life-long:

During this time I was deeply depressed and lonely. I developed rather poor self-esteem and generally thought of the other kids as superior to me. (Sarah)

I felt like an outsider and that no-one would be my friend ... hard to describe ... but I felt alone, and lonely ... (David A.)

I worked really hard to just not care about all the teasing, bullying and humiliation in middle school and high school. (Joseph)

There are emotional scars from all of the years of teasing that I endured. My self-esteem suffered as a result. It took me many years to rebuild that part of myself. (Carol)

David Hawker insisted vehemently:

People at school said things like 'you're weird' and 'there's something wrong with you' – and I agree with them.

Many children, like survivors of trauma, "froze" in response to bullying (I remember being literally unable to move or speak at times) or developed forms of dissociation:

> I pressed my nose to the window and tried to pretend that I wasn't really there, that I wasn't really being teased, etc. This kind of withdrawal and semi-dissociation set up a pattern that would continue for years to come. Well, somehow I managed to learn to bottle up my emotions at least during school. (Karen)

> I would sit there and take it in, even laugh, while they hit me and messed me around. (David Hawker)

> At the age of five or six I felt that my soul was dying and I couldn't stop it or even make anyone understand that anything was wrong. I think that I learned to 'pass' for 'normal' as was expected of me, by dissociating severely. (Joseph)

> I have very strong feelings of horror when I think of school and the way I wasted all those years 'dropping out' while in school so that I can remember very little … I blanked out most of my school days … most of the time I just 'went off somewhere' mentally … (Jack)

> I was on automatic pilot a lot, it must have been, because I don't remember much of my childhood at all … (Gabriela)

In a very few cases that I know of, this dissociation actually became severe enough to lead to a diagnosis of "dissociative identity disorder" (formerly known as "multiple personality disorder").

Many children adopted the strategy of acting "deaf" when social interaction was either too demanding or too frightening, simply not responding to what they heard and/or refusing to speak:

> I 'acted deaf' sometimes. Like when peers were calling me to talk to me and I didn't want to engage in conversation for whatever reason, I would ignore them. One of the reasons might have been a fear of turning my head round if they were sat behind me in the classroom, because then I would be in danger of looking at the other people … what I mean by this is making eye contact with the other people. (David Hawker)

I have observed that children with Asperger's seem to be particularly vulnerable to the effects of bullyindg, often being genuinely traumatized by what others would class as "mild" teasing. My personal theory is that our lack of social understanding reduces the psychological self-defense mechanisms available to us. Most children can interpret a comment like "You're an idiot" in terms of the other's motives ("he's just being mean", "they're saying that to upset me" "she's lying") and so deflect it at least partially from a direct impact on their self-esteem. Often unable even to name what is happening to us as "bullying", children with Asperger's just absorb it, and either feel that we *are* idiots or end up expressing our pain by lashing out.

What schools can do

Dealing with bullying and isolation is one of the most important responsibilities of any school with a pupil with Asperger's syndrome. Extreme bullying – physical or sexual violence – must clearly be addressed through disciplinary action. Similarly, it can and must be made clear that verbal taunting and insults are not acceptable. As Jack wrote:

> Above all, do NOT tolerate other kids making fun of someone who is 'different'. I never could understand why this is so universal. Why do their teachers and parents just let kids do stuff like that? Punish kids who bully others. Especially talk regularly to other kids about tolerating others' differences, no matter if these are social, physical, religious, ethnic, whatever. Never allow other kids to make fun of other kids verbally either.

However, while it is possible to directly prevent children from actually assaulting a classmate with Asperger's, or from teasing them verbally (at least when teachers are around) it is not possible to force them to like them, to play with them, or to choose them as friends. The "no blame" approach (Robinson and Maines, 1997) which aims to make other children aware of the feelings of the child who is being bullied or ostracized (and which, despite the name, makes it clear that responsibility is to be taken by perpetrators and bystanders, not victims) may well have much to offer here, although, as I have already noted, it is hard to build genuine friendships on the basis of pity alone.

It is vital to teach social skills to children with Asperger's, but these must be imparted as factual information, which the child should not be blamed for not knowing in the first place. It is helpful, for example, to explain "If you tell people they are stupid, they will feel hurt and will not want to play with you". It is not helpful to say "How could you be so rude! That was such a mean thing to say … ". Carol Gray's technique of Social Stories (see Edelson, 1995 for a brief account of this method) which creates written scripts outlining behavioural routines for a given situation, can be a very effective strategy.

As Asperger noted, for children with Asperger's syndrome "Social adaptation has to proceed via the intellect. In fact, they have to learn everything via the intellect." (p. 58) In my late teens I started reading books on anthropology, and this was a major breakthrough for me: from then on I had a conceptual framework for studying social rules and beginning to work out how they operated. It is important to recognize that the need to analyse and learn social skills as an academic topic means that they will never come "naturally" or fluently, and not to impose unrealistic and unfair expectations. As Joseph describes:

> People with Asperger's Syndrome are able to learn social norms and rules eventually, but only clumsily and with great intellectual effort, in the way that most people learn mathematics. To us, most normal people, though their obsessions with social interactions which we find irrational and bothersome seems maladaptive to us, are social Mozarts who intuitively learn to employ a very complex set of rules and standards fluidly and creatively, seemingly with little or no effort; we, on the other hand, are stuck with the sheet music, trying to memorize scales and plonking out simple tunes one note at a time.

Ironically, autistic people who are most successful at learning social rules by rote are often also the best at hating themselves for not fitting in and for making mistakes in the first place, and the most vulnerable to the confusing, contradictory and usually negative messages that society sends. So it is particularly important to have support and acceptance when it comes to developing a positive self-image. It's vital to help a child learn social rules if they are going to survive, but it's equally vital to help them understand that there is nothing wrong with them for not knowing these rules in the first place or for finding them illogical and even crazy at times. It needs to be recognized that "acting normal" is never going to be normal or natural for us; Joseph commented that: "one of the most glorious double-binds that [neurotypical people] place on us is the simultaneous injunction to 1) 'Just be yourself' and 2) 'Act NORMAL!'"

It is also important to recognize that children with Asperger's often have a real need for solitude, which at times may be much stronger than their need for contact with others. Social interaction even when desired, is still work, not "break", for children with Asperger's, and breathing space and opportunities for escape are vital. Giving a child permission to have their breaks in the library or designating an office as a "safe place" where they can take refuge when they need quiet can be invaluable.

Interactions with teachers: misreadings

Despite the title of this chapter, the single most important social relationship for a schoolchild with Asperger's syndrome is probably their relationship with the teacher. The significance of the personality of the individual teacher has been recognized ever since Asperger himself wrote that:

> These children often show a surprising sensitivity to the personality of the teacher. However difficult they are even under optimal conditions, they can be guided and taught, but only by those who give them true understanding and genuine affection, people who show kindness towards them and yes, humour. The teacher's underlying emotional attitude influences, involuntarily and unconsciously, the mood and behaviour of the child. (Asperger, 1991, p. 48)

Many children with Asperger's are able to interact far more easily with adults than with other children, especially if those adults are willing to treat them seriously:

> It was easier to talk about my particular interests with educated adults than with children my age. On the last day of school in fourth grade, while the rest of the class was engaged in partying and celebrating, I was busily working out a simplistic proof on identifying the fourth dimension. By comparing the physical dimensions and using some highly visual thinking, I came to the conclusion that the fourth dimension was time. I was so excited by my breakthrough that I ran all over the classroom, happily announcing my discovery, while everyone else paid me no attention. But there were some adults in my neighbourhood who listened to my ramblings, such as a woman in our townhouse complex who sympathetically listened to me as I explained to her my prediction that Mt. Hood would erupt in the following month, based on complicated observations I made on the phases of the moon and the migration of geese during the eruption of Mt. St. Helens. (Sarah)

However, the relationships between children with Asperger's and their teachers are frequently blighted by misunderstanding and misinterpretation. Asperger's could be described as the most invisible of all invisible disabilities; even when a child has been diagnosed, many teachers, however well-meaning, find it hard not to interpret their behaviour as they would that of another child and see them as being intentionally rude, etc.. Peeters and Gillberg explain plausibly that "Rationally, we may understand what it means to suffer from social blindness, but we do not really understand what it means with our heart or guts. We were born with too much social intuition, we simply miss the experience." (1999, p.71) People with Asperger's often seem to act as a sort of "blank canvas" onto which others project their own assumptions and concerns. It is necessary to bear the child's diagnosis in mind constantly and check and re-check one's assumptions. In this process, being aware of particularly common "misreadings" can be helpful.

One common error is to misread the child with Asperger's as "manipulative" or "sneaky". Sometimes, the mannerisms of someone with Asperger's syndrome (which, for example, may include shifting from foot to foot, avoiding eye contact, speaking in a flat and "unconvincing" voice) cause others to perceive us as "shifty" or "trouble" (many people with Asperger's, like me, find that as adults we can't buy something in a shop without being followed around by a security guard, which is ironic given that we are typically painstakingly law abiding).

In particular, avoidance of eye contact causes problems, often leading a teacher to assume mistakenly that a child is not paying attention or is deliberately refusing to meet their gaze. This leads to what I have mentally classed as the "look at me" routine, where a teacher (often when scolding a child) will repeatedly demand "look at me", getting more and more vehement as the child becomes more overloaded and less able to do so (or finally manages to make eye contact with a blank stare, thus usually ensuring that they are incapable of attending to or absorbing the message which the teacher is trying to give them).

Many teachers react with hostility when they see a child apparently usurping their authority by telling off another child who has misbehaved (often in language and tone which may be an uncomfortable mirror of the teacher's own behaviour). It is hard for them to understand that this is logical behaviour for a child who has no innate understanding of hierarchy, and who therefore has learnt by observation that this is what is to be done when rules are broken. As Jim explained, "When I was younger, when I made mistakes people laughed at me so I thought it was what you were supposed to do. I later found out that wasn't the case." The more aware child who has learnt not to scold other children themselves, but to tell a teacher of misbehaviour observed, is equally likely to be seen as a "sneak" for breaking tacit rules about "telling". Yet these behaviours arise from a sincere belief in the rules and an anxious concern that they be kept. It is particularly distressing for children with Asperger's to be told off or ignored when we are trying painfully hard to "be good" and help ensure the rules are kept. Simon commented, "It matters especially what teachers think of me because I respect them as authority figures." If there is a tacit rule that children should not point out each others' misdemeanours to the teacher if they don't directly involve that child, then teachers should be prepared to make this rule explicit (after considering the possible consequences, especially given that a pupil with Asperger's will not be able to distinguish between "important" and "unimportant" breaches of rules).

Children with Asperger's are equally likely to be seen as "rude", "bloodyminded" and "disobedient". Charles wrote that: "I just had the privilege of looking over my primary school files … 'Deviant,' 'delinquent' and 'anti-Christ' were all terms used to describe me." This perception can be due at least in part to manner: my tendency to ask difficult questions in a flat voice that sounded as if I was being sarcastic caused many of my teachers to think that I was being deliberately rude or thought myself superior.

Literal understanding of language could also be a major problem: once, my mother told me that if a teacher said such-and-such to me, I should tell her to go and jump in a lake. Unfortunately I took this completely literally and proceeded to tell the teacher to go and jump in a lake and couldn't work out why she got upset, since I'd been being very good and doing what I was told to do. Similarly, I had been told by everyone that I should tell the truth and that lying was bad, so I couldn't understand why people got upset when I told them they were stupid. Literal understanding of instructions was typically interpreted as sarcasm or "trying to be clever". Teachers found it impossible to understand that an intelligent and apparently verbally fluent child who, told to "pull their socks up!" bent down and pulled their socks up, as David A. did, was not trying to make fun of them, and reactions could be violent:

> When I was seven I had a teacher who used to give me instructions in such a way that if I followed them literally I would be wrong. Then she would slap my hands with a ruler. I didn't understand that until I was about twelve. (Jim)

My major memory of primary school, basically, is of spending a huge amount of time being told off and having no idea why, especially as it seemed to happen when I thought I was being most helpful. It was all fairly Kafka-esque.

Issues of "stubbornness" and "disobedience" often loomed large. In many cases power struggles erupt over issues which are in fact irrelevant or trivial; the teacher's belief that they must be obeyed unquestioningly leads them to refuse to make reasonable concessions or to negotiate. Usually, children with Asperger's find it impossible to understand why "respect for authority" requires that they should do things which are pointless or wrong (even though we may simultaneously be desperate to please others and "be good"). The following story illustrates how such points can become, in a teacher's eyes, major issues of "disrespect" and "disobedience":

> [The teacher] had only one way of doing study skills, time management, etc. and woe unto the person who did not fit her box!! Example: In her opinion, the only way to speed-read was to read with your finger under the line and never read ahead of the finger. The finger was supposed to go faster and faster and faster and hence your reading speed would improve. I was already a speed reader. I, to this day take in words as 'gestalts'. I take in ideas, images, pages, sometimes paragraphs – never a line at a time. Doing something a line at a time is exhausting for me and, because of my visual issues, causes me to lose my place – I quickly

learned to read in a gestalt way as a compensation. I tried to explain that I was a fast reader already and that the technique was not helpful to me. Her response initially was: 'Well, you just need more practice. Even the fastest readers have room for improvement'. After several minutes of frustrating attempts to conform to this stupid technique, which only slowed me down, and kept me from reading all the wonderful things that my eyes were already wandering towards, I would start to just stop using my finger when her back was turned. When she caught me, I was basically lambasted for not respecting her authority. I was bewildered and angry – and saw no use to this technique – so I continued to do the accepted technique when I had to and to stop when I thought that her back was turned. I figured that she just didn't understand and that the point of this was speed reading, so I might as well speed read, instead of waste my time with a technique that didn't work for me. Being disrespectful or 'difficult' was the furthest thing from my mind. Continuing instances like this ended up landing me in the first detention of my life! You must realize that I was usually the 'Miss Goody Two Shoes' of the classroom and so this was pretty emotionally devastating for me. (Karen)

Often, the demands that children with Asperger's make are entirely reasonable ones, which could clearly be accommodated without destroying the structure or discipline of the school; this fact gets ignored when the issue is seen as one of "compliance" and it is deemed that the child needs to "learn how to do what they are told" (in fact, absolute obedience without discussion is not required at university, in employment, or in everyday adult life – unless one lives in a totalitarian state – so I am still baffled as to why it is felt that this is something that it is desirable, let alone necessary, to learn).

In fact, demanding absolute compliance with adult commands and submission is counter-productive and potentially dangerous, especially given how vulnerable to abuse and victimization children with Asperger's already are. Wendy Lawson (1998) illustrates this point when, describing her obedience of a stranger who repeatedly sexually abused her, she explains: "I did know that children did what grown-ups told them to do … All that I can remember thinking was that it was important to do as I was told." (p. 36) On a smaller scale, many children with Asperger's learn to nod and say "yes" when asked "Do you understand now?" after a teacher has wearily explained something again, even when they remain baffled (Wing, 1981, notes that people with Asperger's may develop "a habit of answering 'yes' to any question they do not understand, this being the quickest way to cut short the conversation"). Merely extorting compliance from a child does not ensure that they can or will learn. Some children with Asperger's adopt a strategy of robotic compliance, passively obeying every instruction, never initiating anything or volunteering information, because it makes it more likely that people will leave them alone to get on with their thoughts. The teacher may believe they have "won" because a child does not disobey them; in fact they have lost any opportunity for the child to learn from them.

When a child with Asperger's "inexplicably" refuses to do something, and explodes if pressured to do it, it is a mistake to see them as "throwing a tantrum" in order to get out of something; as I will discuss later, they may well, from their perspective, have their back to the wall. There were times when my "no" was all I had. Gunilla Gerland writes:

> My ability just to go on and never give up was … partly due to the fact that these situations were always about things I thought vital … Quite simply, I couldn't afford to lose. (Gerland, 1997, p. 13)

A third common mistake is to assume since the child with Asperger's looks normal, may be verbally fluent and capable of achieving in some academic areas, "there's nothing wrong with him/her" and so if they do not succeed in other areas, they "must try harder." So genuine difficulties are interpreted as laziness or a refusal to work (this is often exacerbated when a student *does* refuse to "try" for the hundredth time to do a given task, having learnt from bitter experience that they will never succeed). My primary school teachers couldn't understand how I could be brilliant at some subjects, and completely incapable of learning others (I managed to be the last child in my year at school to learn my times tables, a couple of years after everyone else did). They generally assumed that I just wasn't trying or was being stubborn. In secondary school, my consistent inability to learn foreign language vocabulary by rote led to a steady stream of comments along the lines of:

> Clare has not been willing to do the learning which would give her the tools with which to gain more enjoyment from learning a language … (1988)

Sometimes children were punished or held back for their perceived "laziness" and obstinate "refusal to try" (an insistence on endless "remedial" work could itself take on a punitive tone):

> I was nine years old and in grade four when my mother was informed that I would not be allowed to go on to grade five due to the fact that I wasn't trying very hard at reading, writing and anything language-oriented. (Schuyler)

In other cases, just the consistent refusal on the teacher's part to believe that a child was not being lazy or stubborn was enough to erode their self-esteem and faith in their own perceptions:

> It was the thing of 'can do better if he tries'. I felt absolutely f***ing terrible because it became a source of serious ridicule in the end. It was

also a source of serious – ah, I can't explain what exactly, but it left me feeling very lousy about myself and my abilities … I was just left with no help at all … (David A.)

Why couldn't I be more responsible? There was so much potential in me if I just tried harder … etc. (Karen)

For children with Asperger's, our achievements often seem to work against us. The more we succeed in certain areas, the less our teachers are willing to believe that we may be genuinely disabled in other areas. Any achievements are interpreted as proof that we never had any problems in the first place.

Mark concluded:

As far as my teachers were concerned, I was bright but perverse and lazy … My great mistake was in not being mentally retarded.

In addition to the humiliation and suffering caused by continually being blamed for "laziness", constantly being required to do things that you know you can't do disrupts any possible trust in the teacher. As Gunilla Gerland (personal communication) comments:

[If] I don't feel trust in my teacher – the feeling that my teacher knows what I can do and what I can't do and the assignment s/he gives may be difficult but s/he knows that I am able to do it – then it will be even more difficult to motivate me to do some things.

Then there's the "rescue fantasy". In this case, the child is seen as emotionally disturbed and "withdrawn", perhaps abused, and the teacher believes that if only they could establish an emotional relationship with this child, all the other problems would vanish. Many children with Asperger's syndrome are also withdrawn, of course, but it is a mistake to perceive the symptoms of Asperger's syndrome itself as withdrawal or as an "autistic shell" into which the child has retreated. In fact, a teacher's attempt to "reach" a child with great kindness usually appears, to a child with Asperger's, as the teacher's mysteriously talking in a strange, "syrupy" voice and insisting on patting them on the arm or shoulder. When people behaved like this to me, my only thought was how to escape as quickly as possible from this baffling and therefore perhaps dangerous behaviour (it wasn't until the end of my teens that I worked out what the intention behind it was). In particular, for a teacher to respond in an emotional "comforting" way when a child is stressed is often disastrous; a child with Asperger's who is upset or anxious will be having enough trouble handling their own emotions without being expected to process and respond to someone else's (Asperger wisely emphasized that "all educational transactions have to be done with the affect 'turned off'" and that the teacher should not "aim to become loved" (p. 47)).

Friendships with teachers can be good but they are not a substitute for teaching or an educational technique. Emotional relationships are not the priority for people with Asperger's syndrome in the same way that they are for neurotypical people; our need for a safe, comprehensible environment comes first. Often, teachers seem to resent the lack of an emotional response or gratitude for their kindness; they feel rejected and object to being treated "like furniture". Instead, it is vital to recognize the need for a child with Asperger's to interact with and through objects and the exchange of bits of information. Teachers must be prepared to be furniture, and aim to be safe and useful pieces of furniture before any other sort of relationship can develop, if indeed it ever does.

Good teachers

Good experiences with teachers, though much fewer than bad experiences, shone in people's recollections with extraordinary vividness. I remember to this day (although I don't remember their names or faces) the primary school teachers who allowed me to do projects on my obsessions, or gave me permission to stay inside the classroom and read instead of going outside at breaktime. Their thoughtfulness made an overwhelming difference to my life. In secondary school, I had some teachers who were willing to discuss my special interests with me outside class hour and, when I developed an interest in philosophy, one teacher helped arrange for me to have lessons in it at weekends (I later went on to do a degree in philosophy at university). Carol gave the following account of the turning-point in her school life:

> The godsend person was my fifth grade teacher (I was in special ed. part time). She was new to our small school and thankfully did not know better than to try to teach me. I was flunking her class like I had flunked all of my classes up to that point. She took me to the side and worked with me. She took the time to teach me some social skills.

> I went from making straight F's to making straight A's. I had a lot of stuff to catch up on but she took the time to teach me what I had missed. I was allowed to go at my own pace which was a lot faster than the rest of the class came to find out. She taught me the basic rules of games. She also taught me how to keep a journal.

> She had such a gentle way about her. She was one of those kinds of people who was genuine and sincere. She had a way of making me want to do better for myself. I don't ever remember being called stupid or being made to feel dumb in her presence.

> There was no one thing that she did that made me trust her. It was all of the little things she did over the course of the year. For example, I used to

*have to sit at the front of the class right beside the teacher's desk. In her
class, I was allowed to sit along the wall of the classroom in the very back
but it was not quite in the corner of the room. I was able to see everyone
without them seeing me or staring at me.*

*She never embarrassed me by making me get up and answer questions.
She allowed me to read books or color whenever I was bored. I was
allowed the freedom to be myself which made me more willing to tolerate
what was going on around me. By the end of that year, I had a quasi-
friend with whom I played. The friendship was arranged by my teacher
with another girl that was very shy and new to the school.*

*After getting the results from a GMAT test where I scored at above
college level in all the scoring areas, she requested an IQ test which took
me out of special ed. and placed me in the gifted and talented program.
This small act made it possible for me to have a wide range of freedom
for the rest of my school years. I was allowed to study what I wanted to
when I wanted to. In high school, I tutored my older brother and sister in
their physics and chemistry classes even though I hadn't had those
courses yet. I was allowed to come and go in the classes as I pleased so
long as I maintained straight A's. If it wasn't for this teacher, I would
probably still be considered retarded and stuck in some institution
somewhere. I owe her my deepest thanks. She caught a lot of flack by my
parents for showing interest in helping me but I'm so glad she did.*

Peeters and Gillberg suggest that, in order to help pupils with Asperger's
syndrome, teachers must be a little different from the norm themselves and that
one key element is an attraction to Asperger's syndrome. Some teachers are
naturally drawn towards working with children with autism and Asperger's
syndrome, while others are not:

*It is useless to 'force' someone to work with autistic children (we know
examples where directors randomly appoint teachers and it just does not
work). Professionals must choose autism themselves. They do not choose
'in spite of autism', but 'because of autism.' ... we have always said, for
want of another explanation, that one needs to be bitten by the bug of
autism. For insiders, this is perfectly clear. We know professionals who will
never be bitten by the bug – who are immune to it. The problem is that
bugs are invisible to the authorities. (Peeters and Gillberg, 1999, p. 82–3)*

Among the key characteristics needed by a teacher of children with
Asperger's, they list being attracted to differences and the unknown, the ability to
"give without getting an (ordinary) thank you" and "to be willing to adapt one's

natural style of communication and social interaction". The best teachers, I would suggest, also seem to have a genuine enjoyment and appreciation of the quirks of children with Asperger's syndrome. When it comes to classroom manner and practical techniques of teaching, Asperger's recommendations from 1944 are still valid today:

> *The teacher must at all costs be calm and collected and must remain in control. He should give his instructions in a cool and objective manner, without being intrusive. A lesson with such a child may look easy and appear to run in a calm, self-evident manner. It may even seem that the child is simply allowed to get away with everything, any teaching being merely incidental. Nothing could be further than the truth. In reality, the guidance of these children requires a high degree of effort and concentration. The teacher needs a particular inner strength and confidence which is not at all easy to maintain! (Asperger, p. 48)*

Carol, who described her "godsend" teacher, also wrote a manifesto outlining the qualities and knowledge that she believed were needed for good teachers and fellow students; I feel it is worth quoting in full:

> *The issues I find most important for teachers and students alike are tolerance, acceptance, understanding and a willingness to learn. Teachers and students should learn tolerance for an autistic individual's differences whether it may be the noises that they make, the hard time they have with language, or any of the other autistic traits. Autistics should be allowed to be themselves and not be looked down upon for being different. Teachers should show tolerance of an autistic child's unique capabilities, self-stimulations, repetitive behavior, and so forth. On the same token, teachers should practice zero-tolerance for any teasing, joke, or harassment of the autistic child or at the autistic child's expense.*

> *Teachers and students need to learn that acceptance is more than tolerance. They need to value the diversity that an autistic child brings to the classroom. Autistic children should be accepted for who they are, with their strengths and weaknesses intact.*

> *Teachers and students need to understand that an autistic child is not merely a child that needs more discipline. They need to know what autism is and isn't. They also need to understand that they will not be able to make this child non-autistic. The teachers and students need to be taught compassion.*

Teachers need to demonstrate an active willingness to learn. They should be taught from the beginning that they will never become experts on teaching autistic children as there has not been a proven method of teaching that is perfect for every autistic child. They should be willing to try new things and to 'think outside of the box.' These teachers may become experienced with working with autistic children, but that is far from being an expert. They need to keep open lines of communication with the parents as this is extremely crucial to the child's overall development at home and at school.

6
In the Lunch Queue: the sensory and motor environment

This chapter is entitled "In the Lunch Queue" because the lunch queue is a key example of a daily feature of school which sensory problems can turn into a nightmare, but which is rarely even considered in discussions of education. The importance of school as a sensory/motor environment is rarely considered and so the idea that something as ordinary as a lunch queue could be a source of major stress for a child with Asperger's syndrome rarely even occurs to neurotypical people.

Sensory problems at school

The corridors and halls of almost any mainstream school are a constant tumult of noises echoing, fluorescent lights (a particular source of visual and auditory stress for people on the autistic spectrum), bells ringing, people bumping into each other, the smells of cleaning products and so on. For anyone with the sensory hyper-sensitivities and processing problems typical of an autistic spectrum condition, the result is that we often spend most of our day perilously close to sensory overload (the only everyday sensory experience that neurotypical people have that is remotely similar seems to be "rush hour"). Like computers overloaded with information and required to process too much at one time, we often "crash". Some people shut down and "tune out" completely:

> Sometimes if there was too much commotion around me, either in movement of people or in noise, I would just automatically tune out. In situations such as these, my senses would sometimes not be integrated and each individual sound would be heard crisply as a separate sound and each visual detail would clutter my line of sight. So I would just stare blankly without exactly looking at anything and I would sometimes not be aware if I happened to be looking in the direction towards someone. I would often not be aware of anything during these episodes and would even not notice if someone was trying to get my attention. (Sarah)

Noise levels were a common source of stress; Darius commented "If your sensory system doesn't work too well, lots of distracting sounds are very tiring."

Being in close physical proximity to others is a particular problem for some people with Asperger's and deliberately arriving at lessons early in order to capture a seat on an aisle or in a corner was a common strategy (others felt safest if they could be near a door or window). Physical proximity could be a serious problem during exams and tests:

> [The thing that was most difficult about school was] being so physically close to the other kids … trying to concentrate when they had all the kids sit at one big table a few inches from each other and take aptitude-type tests … (Jack)

School assemblies, narrow corridors and lunch queues were very stressful for the same reason and some people ended up lashing out if pushed or jostled. Simply navigating through a crowd could cause problems of spatial and social disorientation:

> I walk fast and when walking on the pavement by the road I would often come up to a group of slower walkers. I found it very difficult to navigate around them, was too shy to ask them to let me through. So I just slowed my pace and hung to the back of them until we got to a space where there was room for me to overtake. This all made me feel very awkward. (David Hawker)

All through secondary school, I would wait until the very end of lunchbreak, when there would only be a few people left in the queue, to get my lunch and on some days I would be unable to face it at all. Allowing a child to "queue-jump", to have a seat on an aisle in exams, or to always sit in the same seat in the classroom, could make a remarkable difference to their ability to cope. Simply making sure that a child has access to "sensory retreats" during the day (being able to spend time in a quiet library, for example) can make a dramatic difference.

More subtle problems (as opposed to sheer volume of sensory input) include disorientation: many people with Asperger's have great difficulty finding their way around school, even after following a route with their class group many times. At the age of ten, after being at the same school for five years, I still couldn't find my way around it. Often, we have trouble creating a mental map of our environment without being shown an actual map to provide a visual image, and we do not always recognize the cues that others use to navigate:

I spent a whole year in highschool before realising that room number 303 means the room is on the third floor (300) and in the left wing (odd numbers). When I was in kindergarten we had to hang up our coats always at the same peg and put our ... wellingtons underneath it, in order to avoid confusion when school was over. I did this by some sort of spatial navigation, rather like blind people use. I entered the hall and than walked under a certain angle towards the [pegs] on the wall. I would end up before the one I always used (other kids never told me I'd hung my stuff on their peg, so I assume it worked). One day a little boy asked me what my 'picture' was. I hadn't got a clue what he was talking about. So he asked me: well, don't you know where to hang your coat then? Of course I do, I replied rather indignantly. I had to prove that I did, so I went to the hall with him and sort of zeroed in on 'my' coat-peg. Oh, you've got a toadstool he said. And sure enough, there was a picture of a toadstool pasted above my peg. I didn't see why that was so important to him. Only recently did it dawn on me that the child-carers probably put those pictures there so children would know where to hang their coats. (Darius)

This could result in panic and "inexplicable" refusal when a child was told "go to the staffroom" or "take this to the office". Jim remembered:

Once, after one of the many times when I was sent to the office for misbehaviour, the principal walked me out the north door of the school (I usually exited from the south-east door). Though I had lived in the neighborhood for four or five years, I was totally disoriented.

It is often forgotten that non-teaching staff, such as dinner ladies, also need to be informed about Asperger's syndrome. Often, situations outside formal lessons are equally or more demanding for the child with Asperger's. Lunch, again, is a good example, since it could be difficult for many reasons in addition to the lunch queue.

Simply understanding the tacit rules of the situation could be extremely difficult. Do you need to get a tray? If you forget, can you go and get one? Do you serve yourself with food or do you have to ask (for some people, having to choose food "on the spot" was very difficult)? Can you choose where to sit or do you have to sit at a certain table? When you finish, do you have to put your plate and tray away in a certain place? The potential for making mistakes (and the anxiety caused by the fear of making mistakes) is enormous. One of my most vivid memories of secondary school is of being hauled out of the lunch queue by one of the dinner ladies, shouting angrily, and made to stand to one side; she refused to tell me why – "You know what you've been doing". Only after I had burst into tears was I allowed back into the queue; nobody ever explained what I'd done wrong in the first place and to this day I still have no idea.

For some people, just having to eat while in a crowded and noisy environment made them feel exposed and vulnerable. David Hawker (who pointed out the similarity of some elements of his behaviour to social phobia) wrote:

> ... there were some problems with my eating/drinking. I would never be seen dead doing it at first - they had to let me into the disabled toilet to get privacy to drink. Then I started going to the canteen, which I found very scary, though fortunately I asked a good friend if I could go in with him and we went together - after that it wasn't so bad and I got used to it. Eating alone most of the time ... a few times other students came and tried to talk to me, which was of course very traumatic ... then I eventually stopped going and took packed lunches instead, by the time I got to A-level. If I remember correctly I went up to the 6th form study room to eat ... I didn't want to eat it in the common room. I found privacy was always important for eating.

Sensory problems with taste, smell and texture could make certain foods intolerable and this could cause enormous problems in schools where children were expected to finish everything on their plate. One of the worst features of my primary school was being expected to drink a bottle of milk, warm from standing all day; I nearly vomited on a regular basis. Many children with Asperger's can only eat certain foods prepared in a certain manner (Sarah remembered "I would ... require the food on my plate to not touch each other and I always ate each item at a time instead of mixed together") and may prefer to eat exactly the same thing each day.

For some people, lavatories are a special refuge, the only place in a school where privacy and solitude are possible (as long as you learn to cry silently):

> I would retreat to the restroom for a secure place to be. I felt good with the sound of water running and I would be rocking and making mouth movements; AND once in a while make my favorite same words. So the restroom was a place to let out my world a little bit where there was nobody else in there and I can get security and privacy. A lot of the times I would ask the teacher if I could use the bathroom. (Leah)

But they can also be sources of fear and stress, for both sensory reasons – shiny white ceramics, loud echoes, smells – and social reasons: in many schools, lavatories are places where bullies can easily corner someone away from teachers' eyes.

Sensory problems could mean that bodily signals such as hunger, thirst or the need to urinate were not registered, or were only registered at the last moment. Karen explained: "I ... did not gain full bladder control until around 11, when I stopped having to wear "adult diapers" to bed every night." Teachers who refused to allow a child to leave lessons to go to the lavatory ("You should have thought of that at breaktime") could be a source of great stress. For most of secondary school, I tried to deal with this problem by not drinking any water during the day, even though this meant I often choked while eating.

Motor problems

Motor problems create another huge area of difficulty, which loomed large in the recollection of many people with Asperger's. Many people with autism have clumsy or awkward movements, almost certainly due to differences in the cerebellum. This can cause problems in a number of areas, notably with handwriting (Asperger noted rather wearily of one of his cases, "Like almost all autistic individuals, this ... boy had atrocious handwriting." [Asperger, p. 63]) and PE, as well as resulting in an odd, "robotic-looking" way of moving which is a common target for teasing. However, in the absence of an identified physical disability, this is rarely acknowledged as a genuine inability: instead, poor handwriting is considered "messiness" or "sloppiness" and cause for endless time spent "remedially" tracing letters (instead of being allowed to type or use a computer, or even to accept legible but messy handwriting). As an adult, I still can't do joined-up handwriting – I learnt how to make some of my letters join, but not others, and I ended up simply printing letters very close together. Very slow handwriting may cause difficulty when taking dictation or making notes:

> I often had problems finishing my 'dictation'. I write really slowly (and illegibly) so I only was able to write half of the sentences read by the teacher. I mean, I wrote half of the sentence and then went on to the (first half) of the next sentence and so on. Then, after he'd finished dictating he'd stand next to my desk wrestling to get my dictation paper from me, which I guarded with my life, whilst furiously scribbling the second half of the dictation-sentences after the unfinished first halves. I always had straight A's. As I said, I have a great memory. (Darius)

School sports were spontaneously mentioned by almost everyone I interviewed as one of the worst features of school, combining as they did demands on physical co-ordination, sensory processing and social abilities:

> I never was good at sports. My dad tried to force-teach me catch and baseball, but I hated it with a passion and could never catch or hit, as my hand-eye co-ordination was terrible ... I was always the last kid to get

picked for any teams in gym class and was even put in 'special ed. gym class' with the mentally retarded kids in 1st grade. I got along with them, but hated the taunting that I got by my phys. ed. teacher and some of my fellow 'normal' classmates in regular gym. (Fred)

Despite difficulty with social understanding, children with Asperger's are often very sensitive to humiliation, and sports activities (and the associated social interaction in locker rooms) were a rich source of this:

I finally was walking and talking by around 6 or 7, but sports and co-ordination were the nemesis of my life … P.E. was the ultimate in social embarrassment. To this day, I still get a bit wary and paranoid in locker rooms, because they remind me of the constant teasing and the 'ugly duckling' feelings I experienced. (Karen)

During years of tennis lessons, I literally never once succeeded in serving a tennis ball, and only managed to "shoot" a ball into a basket once or twice (only in practices, never in an actual game of netball). P.E. teachers made no accommodations to a student who genuinely couldn't hit a ball, turn a somersault or do front crawl (I was terrified and overloaded by anything that required me to be upside-down or put my face in water; given my poor co-ordination, I think this actually displayed an excellent instinct for self-preservation) except to tell me to do it again and try harder. After spending an hour swinging a tennis racket at a ball which I couldn't track, or choking on chlorinated water for the umpteenth time, I only felt more of a failure then ever.

As well as purely physical problems, auditory processing problems could make following a string of instructions almost impossible:

I find it difficult to take spoken instructions – e.g. in P.E. I didn't know what to do like in activities where you have to jump through hoops and move bean bags around and stuff. (David Hawker)

Comprehension of the rules of sports (spoken and unspoken) is also a major problem:

On another occasion, I ran in a relay race, only to abruptly stop midway to pick a flower and sniff it – seemingly oblivious that a race was going on. (Sarah)

By the time I left school, I still had no idea of the rules of tennis, as it had been assumed that everybody knew them and so they had never been explained. I understood that I had to hit the ball over the net, but had no idea whether I was supposed to be trying to hit it so that the other person could hit it back or so that they couldn't. Since I never managed to hit the ball in any case, the question remained purely academic, but I was still left feeling stupid and too ashamed to ask.

Team sports were the worst source of humiliation, with students with Asperger's invariably being the last picked for any team:

> *Because of my poor motor co-ordination and disinterest in games and sports, I was considered very unreliable in P.E. When we played kickball, I was always put in the outfield which isolated me from everyone else – and I proceeded to enter my own imaginary world. I often pretended that the grassy area I was standing on was some other country and would imagine what it would look like. At first I didn't understand what I was supposed to do out there. Later when I did learn, I had already developed quite a bit of resentment towards the other kids too, so that if the ball ever came my way I would always ignore it – which, of course, only reinforced my reputation as an unreliable P.E. participant. (Sarah)*

The swimming pool could also be a source of sensory stress (Gabriela mused "not sure if it was presence of other kids in there, lights, noise, not being able to reach the bottom ..."). Many people couldn't tolerate water splashing on their face (avoiding showers for this reason), let alone putting their face under water:

> *For me, swimming in gym class was the most traumatic experience of high school. (I still can't swim, by the way). (Thomas)*

> *I hated and feared swimming lessons. I can't remember why, unfortunately. I know the instructor yelled at me but again, I can't remember why. However, it may very well have been a water in the face problem. I no longer mind water on the face but still cannot swim because I cannot coordinate my arm movements and my breathing. (Vicky)*

> *However, some people reported greatly enjoying swimming later when it was on their own terms (now I love swimming, but then, now I also decide when to go in the water, when to go out ... what to do in there ... it's different). (Gabriela)*

The National Curriculum requirements for P.E., which, for example, stipulate that at Key Stage 2 (for 7–11 year olds) "Pupils should be taught ... to understand and play small-sided games and simplified versions of recognised competitive team and individual games, covering the following types – invasion, e.g. mini-soccer, netball, striking/fielding, e.g. rounders, small-sided cricket, net/wall, e.g. short tennis ... common skills and principles, including attack and defence, in invasion, striking/fielding, net/wall and target games … [and] to improve the skills of sending, receiving, striking and travelling with a ball in the above games," seem, from the perspective of a person with Asperger's syndrome, more like punishment or torture than anything else. There is no conceivable way that I or anybody with Asperger's syndrome I know could master these skills as adults, let alone aged 11, and nobody I interviewed could see any point whatsoever in compelling students with Asperger's to participate in sports against their will:

> If a kid does not want to play team or other sports, he/she should not be forced to either. Teachers used to chase me out into the field and try to make me play sports. I wanted only to swing and play on the monkey bars. (Jack)

If it is deemed necessary for students with Asperger's to participate in compulsory P.E. of some sort, then surely this could be an opportunity to teach non-competitive activities which may later become solitary leisure skills, such as walking, and/or which develop body awareness and relaxation skills, such as yoga. When voluntary and suited to individual needs and interests, physical activities could sometimes be a positive way for people with Asperger's to explore and begin to develop confidence in an area (bodily control and coordination) in which we often feel particularly vulnerable and unsure (with good reason). Darius hypothesized that children with Asperger's might naturally seek out the experiences they needed:

> I spent my childhood standing on my head more than on my feet and learning to do such things like walking a tightrope, juggling balls and the like (I was passionate about the circus). I think I knew quite well I needed the experience in order to get better at 'seeing' and co-ordination. When I saw a ballet class in action in the old gymnastics building, I immediately knew that I wanted to do that as well. I could hardly see what was going on, but I was absolutely sure that I needed to be in that class …

It is therefore particularly sad that our experience of P.E. at school is usually the exact opposite, undermining our confidence further and leaving us with even more experiences of clumsiness, fear, pain and incompetence.

7
Secondary conditions and challenging behaviour

Often, secondary problems, such as "co-morbid" neurological conditions, or emotional and behavioural problems, can be as much of, or more of, a problem as Asperger's itself. Certain psychiatric conditions are more common in people with Asperger's than in the rest of the population and it can be vital to be able to recognize and cope with them.

Neurological "clustering"

It has been suggested that Asperger's may be part of a larger "cluster" of neurological conditions and studies have shown that significant numbers of people with Asperger's also show signs of attention-deficit/hyperactivity disorder, obsessive-compulsive disorder (characterized by recurrent, unwanted and intrusive thoughts or impulses – for example, a compulsion to wash the hands repeatedly, or to touch a doorway twenty times in a ritualized manner before being able to pass through it), or Tourette's syndrome (characterized by motor or vocal tics such as jerking or barking – although Tourette's is most notorious for coprolalia, involuntary swearing, this is actually only present in around 10% of cases). Some people with Asperger's also have specific learning difficulties such as dyslexia or dyscalculia and people with autistic spectrum conditions as a group display higher than average rates of epilepsy.

Too often, one diagnosis (such as Asperger's syndrome) is assumed to rule out the possibility of other concurrent problems and so it is vital that teachers and others are aware that not only does having Asperger's syndrome not make one somehow immune to other conditions, it may even make them slightly more likely than average. The presence of one diagnosis should not mask the possibility of others.

Depression and anxiety

The stresses of living with Asperger's syndrome (some of which I hope I have adequately described) undeniably and unsurprisingly create a higher risk of emotional disorders and teachers can play an essential role in recognizing and alleviating some of these pressures. Ironically, there is some research evidence that the milder an autistic spectrum condition is, the more likely it is that the person will have problems with depression, anxiety and so forth (this is also borne out by my personal experience and observations). A socially-oblivious, "aloof" autistic child is likely to be immune to many of the social messages which indicate that their behaviour is unacceptable, while a more socially aware and verbally able child can be desperately vulnerable to them (many "low-functioning" autistic people have a sense of integrity and confidence in who they are that I envy; the world is often confusing and frustrating for them, but they will never come to believe that it is they and not the world who are at fault).

My personal estimate is that at least half of all people with Asperger's syndrome suffer from clinical depression at some point in their lives, often starting during the teens. Wing (1981) reports that one follow-up study of 22 people with Asperger's found that 5 (nearly a quarter) had attempted suicide by early adult life. Several people I interviewed had "breakdowns" in their early teens, often featuring uncontrollable crying, which often marked the start of years of depression. Often these resulted from years of erosion of self-esteem, but were then triggered by apparently trivial issues or erupted out of "nowhere". David A. wrote:

Nervous breakdown at 12 ... It was after I got hanged, a 'friend' decided to take the piss out of me all the way home about my end of term grades, and I walked into the house. I didn't respond to anything said to me, but my mum asked if I was alright and I just burst into tears.

It is important for teachers to be on the lookout for signs that something may be wrong: the quiet and passive child is not necessarily okay. Like many people with Asperger's, my ability to use my face and voice to convey emotion is dependent on my being in a relatively good frame of mind — when I am stressed, my voice will typically become flatter and my face expressionless, so that I may seem to be calm (conversely, it is not unknown for people to misread the behaviour of a happy child with Asperger's as indicating distress or boredom).

Some children will react to intolerable stresses at school by "freezing" during school hours and then exploding in response to the slightest problem at home. Consequently, when parents' reports of a child's behaviour at home differ radically from that child's behaviour at school, teachers should not assume that parents' observations are unreliable, nor complacently attribute it to their superior "behaviour management" skills and the parents' presumed inability to "handle" their child.

Counselling with a practical focus, such as cognitive-behavioural therapy, can help to challenge negative thoughts and self-image and develop positive strategies for coping, but it is vital that any therapist have a good understanding of Asperger's syndrome. A number of people had bad experiences with psychotherapists who failed to identify Asperger's or who took a psychoanalytic line to autistic problems and who were generally felt to be worse than useless. Sometimes their "help" was wholly irrelevant to the concerns and problems of the child with Asperger's:

> At age ten or eleven, someone was so alarmed by the morbidity of my sense of humour on a 'creative writing' test that I took (reading it now, it really is a lot more morbid than funny) that they told my parents (I wasn't told) that I was potentially suicidal. I saw a psychologist weekly for a year or two, but it was a waste of time. (Joseph)

> When I was 7 and still very isolated, spending much of my time rocking in solitude and going through stereotypical touching routines, a paediatrician suggested I might be mildly autistic. Unfortunately I was then passed on to a pair of pseudo-Freudian psycho-charlatans who didn't think autism was a helpful concept and were more interested in what I might have seen in the woodshed as a little boy. Of this time I have clearer memories. It was a dismal failure. They spent two years trying to coerce me every week into playing and talking. I spent two years staring fixedly out the window every week, because I didn't get the point of it and all I knew was that they were suggesting there was something wrong with me. Eventually they gave up and announced that I would grow out of it. This was a triumph of a kind for me. One thing I have never lacked is sheer bloody-minded persistence. (Mark)

In other cases, therapists would attempt to tackle problems of anxiety or depression without referring to the very real factors in that person's life which were often responsible for making them anxious or depressed in the first place; Elizabeth reported that as an adult:

> I would see someone for the mood stuff and I would get over the depression and they would say "okay, you're better now." But, the cause wasn't dealt with and I knew that this was a problem, and that it would come again.

In other cases, therapy which blamed the person for causing their own social failure (by "withdrawing" or unconsciously making others reject them) could actually erode self-esteem even further and undermine the person's ability to trust their own perceptions. I spent most of my teens fairly consistently depressed, because I couldn't (and often didn't want to) do any of the things my classmates were doing, like making friends or being invited to parties or having boyfriends, and I was socially aware enough to realize that this made me a failure and a freak. I ended up being seen by the doctor about my depression. As I never came across anyone who knew about Asperger's syndrome, the doctor (who of course only saw me being articulate in his office and never saw me floundering trying to cope with the simplest social conversation at school) assumed that my social problems were imaginary – the result of my depression. I was briefly sent to a psychotherapist, who helpfully informed me that all of my problems were the result of my being sexually repressed. I stopped going after six sessions, but a lot of damage was still done to my self-esteem, as everyone seemed to be telling me that I was subconsciously causing all my problems myself.

Anxiety disorders are a major problem for many people with Asperger's. This seems to be partly biological in nature. Permanently high anxiety levels have long been noted as common in autistic spectrum conditions, they are often "free-floating" and not associated with any identifiable object and they sometimes seem to be exacerbated by hormonal changes (many people report that attacks of anxiety suddenly appeared or became worse at puberty). They can also overlap with obsessive-compulsive behaviour – for example, I sometimes display mild obsessive-compulsive symptoms such as having to repeatedly return to check that the front door is closed, or that the gas is off, I have my keys, I have all my things in my bag, etc.. As a child I would often have to get out of bed at night to make sure that stacks of books in my room were lined up "properly" (at exact right angles). Anxiety can also be associated with perseveration and "stuck" thinking: I can end up going on and on and on at people when I'm worried that they may not understand, or do exactly what they say they will. However, it also seems clear that biological tendencies to high levels of anxiety can only be exacerbated by living in an environment which, as viewed by a child with Asperger's, is often terrifyingly chaotic and unpredictable.

In some cases, medication can be very helpful in managing permanently high levels of anxiety and/or severe depression, and both recent research and the personal experience of many people with Asperger's suggest that the SSRIs (the group of drugs including Prozac) may be particularly effective in controlling obsessive worrying in people with autistic spectrum conditions (this is so for me personally). However, medication is a very individual issue in more ways than one; not only do different people feel very differently about the idea of pharmaceutically altering their mental state, but people on the autistic spectrum are particularly prone to idiosyncratic responses to medications. Some people require a much lower-than-usual dose of any medication, while others find that severe side-effects outweigh any benefits. Some display "paradoxical" reactions (for example, becoming "hyper" in response to sedatives). Although medication must of course be prescribed by a doctor, it is important for teachers and other school professionals to have a basic awareness of such issues since they may be involved in identifying a need for medication in the first place and in monitoring (and sometimes taking the brunt of) the effects.

"Challenging behaviour"

In some ways, separating "challenging behaviour" in children from Asperger's syndrome from depression and anxiety is an artificial distinction; they are often closely intertwined. David A. emphasized that:

Behavioural problems will occur in a child who doesn't have any other means of attracting attention to his/her discomfort/insecurity about any specific situation …

While some people were exceptionally punctual and diligent in their attendance (David Hawker remembered "I always went for compulsory lessons, despite all the bullying etc."), several people developed "school refusal" at one point or another, in my view unsurprisingly given how traumatic and terrifying school could be. Asked for his most vivid memories of his schooldays, Jim responded:

Fear. Fear of making a mistake. Fear of people laughing at me once I realized what it meant. Fear of hurting someone because I got upset and couldn't deal with it. Fear of being in a place where almost nothing made sense. It was so bad that I would use any excuse to avoid school.

Many cases of "school refusal" included psychosomatic illness. Alice wrote:

I used to go through very, very elaborate feigned illnesses just to keep me from going to school. I pretended I couldn't walk for a while. For a while, I just screamed, cried and threw a fit even if it meant being regarded as a psychiatric basket case as long as it would keep me out of school. At one point, I claimed I couldn't see my work. It goes on. It wasn't worth the trouble I caused me and the fuss I made in response to push me into going to school.

However, she added:

This isn't to say that I didn't feel legitimately physically ill by going to school. I was in just about as much misery as any could have been for most of my school years. I should have had my right to respectfully say 'no'.

Joseph emphasized:

I wasn't pretending to be sick, I really was sick. I was sick and light-headed and couldn't attend to anything, in part because school was so traumatic for me that I was willing to do anything to get out of it.

Darius remembered as an inter-connected whole:

Depression, migraine and migraine equivalents, being sick every morning before school, not being able to eat because of feeling nauseous, not belonging, boredom, feeling that we were learning a lot of crap and essential stuff was left out. Having suicidal thoughts, wanting to run away …

For many people, just getting through "everyday" activities and being around people continuously produced extreme fatigue and exhaustion; Alice commented that "being around people generally tires me out" and Jack remembered being "in a state of incredible tenseness all day" throughout his school days. In my teens, I developed chronic fatigue syndrome for several years and was able to be in school only intermittently. Given that school also caused clinical depression and anxiety for many, it is clear that a distinction between real and feigned illness in these cases cannot be maintained. It is not useful to treat schoolchildren with AS who become ill in this way as "deceitful" or "manipulative"; instead, where illness cannot be tied to a physical cause, professionals need to look at the stresses and pressures it may indicate.

It's vital to address the reasons for any form of problem behaviour, rather than simply aiming to "manage" or "modify" it. Karen commented:

I have nothing against the concept of behavior modification, as long as the human being and their needs and unique quirks don't get lost in the process. However, my experience of it, whether the teachers intended it that way or not, was negative and dehumanizing.

Dr. Ross Greene (1998) has pointed out that behavioural approaches which rely on rewards and punishments can only work to motivate someone to do what they are capable of doing; they cannot provide someone with the cognitive tools necessary to be able to control their behaviour at times of stress, tools "including mental flexibility, the ability to shift from one mind-set to another, problem solving, planning, organizing one's thoughts and controlling one's impulses" (p. 13).

He suggests that many children with neurologically-based conditions, such as severe ADHD, Tourette's, OCD, bipolar disorder or the autistic spectrum conditions, display what he calls "inflexible-explosive" behaviour: lacking some or all of these tools, they become "stuck" when confronted with a problem and, if others fail to intervene to help resolve the problem, or inadvertently escalate the situation, move into a vicious circle of increasing stress and decreasing ability to think flexibly and rationally, until "meltdown" occurs.

His descriptions fit the "meltdowns" that I and others experienced with great accuracy. Often, we would fall apart with great rapidity under stress, moving within a very short space of time from being apparently articulate and controlled to hitting, screaming, swearing and running away. At such times rote-learnt skills, such as eye-contact, social skills, ability to cope with changes in routine and verbal ability will often disintegrate (at times of great stress, I literally become monosyllabic, drop all eye-contact and start "wandering" away from anyone I'm near), thus diminishing options for coping even further:

> ... one time, I just ran off and hid in an empty classroom far away from the one my lesson was in ... (David A.)

> I used to call it 'going ballistic'. One time I walked out of a class and didn't return for a week ... I fought a lot. A lot. Sometimes I would be so out of control I would skip school. I learned to hide out in the photographic darkroom, and to find places where I could control the stimuli. I got into a lot of trouble. (Jim)

It's worth noting here that aggression towards others can sometimes be associated with paranoia. A natural tendency towards self-centredness plus difficulty interpreting the motives of others may make it very hard to understand that others are not "out to get you" when so much of what they do is frightening and distressing (I once ended up saying "f*** you" to several complete strangers in the school library in the belief that they were deliberately talking loudly in order to prevent me from reading). It becomes even harder to develop an accurate perception of what is going on when, some of the time, others genuinely are ganging up on and persecuting you, as happens to so many children with Asperger's (at one point in my teens, I became very scared that I was going mad, since, among other things, I was convinced that everyone was talking about me behind my back, which I knew from my extensive reading could be a sign of schizophrenia; years later, I found out from a schoolmate that the other children in my class had indeed discussed me and my peculiarities quite extensively behind my back).

Self-injurious behaviour (including hand-biting, head-banging and hitting the head with a hand) was usually rarer than in people with more severe autism, but also occurred, sometimes in secret. Escalating sensory hypersensitivities during a meltdown could mean that the body, as well as being a handy target for venting rage and distress on, would start to feel like something attached to or trapping you: self-injury can provide a controllable physical sensation to focus on and shut out some of the overload.

Temple Grandin (1995, p. 44) has usefully compared meltdowns to epileptic fits, which can't be stopped once they have started, but must be allowed to run their course. It's helpful to see what is going on as a sort of "brainstorm" rather than blaming the person in question for not being able to control themselves or dismissing them as "throwing a tantrum" or "attention-seeking". Often it's possible to intervene in the early stages, but once a meltdown has really got going, nothing is likely to get through.

Karen's account illustrates how pressures from the environment combined with the vulnerabilities associated with Asperger's syndrome could make "explosions" almost inevitable:

> I still had a very low frustration tolerance. Sensory overload was a daily thing – sights, sounds, emotions, lights and touch were all experienced intensely and I was easily overwhelmed by what to others would seem like the simplest task. Difficulties in sequencing – i.e. seeing activities and interactions in steps persisted. I would lose two or three steps in a conversation or activity and then be perceived as anti-social or not trying hard enough. What complicated things is that I could do things like write stories or draw great pictures and otherwise give off the impression of being more 'neurotypical' than I actually was and then it would all break down for me with things like household chores or remembering basic hygiene or getting my 'going to bed' routine done. Or just 'common sense' social interactions at school. So periodically, at school and at home, the stress would build up and I would explode. Classic case of the straw that broke the camel's back.

It is vital to look at a child's behaviour in relation to the demands being made on them by the environment and to consider whether some of these demands are really necessary. Patricia Howlin (1998, p. 200) notes that when it comes to improving challenging behaviour: "letting [children] spend play/game times alone in the library or carrying out other tasks and providing them with a set place to sit may all have much greater impact than a complex behavioural programme."

Some teachers are reluctant to make such allowances on the grounds that they won't "solve" the child's behavioural problems ("they have to learn to behave"). Obviously, such concessions on their own won't help a child develop better coping strategies, but the fact that they are not sufficient does not mean that they are not necessary. While it is important to teach a child how to cope with their feelings in more productive and flexible ways, they will never be able to learn if teachers' own behaviour continually pushes them over the edge of what they can cope with. Greene (1998) emphasizes the need to make a child's environment tolerable for them before work can begin on building new cognitive skills. Nobody can begin to learn, let alone master, difficult new coping skills, if they are permanently at breaking point.

8
Preparing for life after school

While the idea of "early intervention" in autism attracts a lot of attention, many people with Asperger's, like me, find that the most critical period in our lives begins in our teens (Kanner 1973, noted that the children he studied who became successful as adults often seemed to reach a turning point in their early-to-mid teens) and continues into our twenties and even thirties. In many ways, we are late bloomers, often reaching our social and emotional "adolescence" a decade or more later than our "peers". Consequently, it is ludicrous to assume that the education of someone with Asperger's is over when they are sixteen or eighteen, and it is vital to ensure that support and opportunities for development and learning continue. Many people with Asperger's need the transition from living at home to living and working independently to be very gradual in order to make the transition successfully and higher or further education or training can be an important way of bridging the gap.

For some people, academic ability will make university an option. Although the idea of someone with an autistic spectrum condition attending university often produces an incredulous reaction, researchers ever since autism was first defined have noted that a small minority of people with autistic spectrum conditions do go to university.

Hans Asperger's 1944 paper mentioned that one of his patients had not only studied theoretical astronomy at university, but also proved a mathematical error in Newton's work and went on to a promising academic career. In 1966, Lorna Wing and J. K. Wing (1981) mentioned that they knew of one young man with autism who was at university. Leo Kanner (1973), who discovered "early infantile autism", reported that of the 96 patients diagnosed as autistic at the Children's Psychiatric Clinic of the John Hopkins Psychiatric Hospital before 1953, by 1972 one had "excelled in mathematical physics on a scholarship at Columbia University", one had done "exceptionally well in college", Thomas G. went to John Hopkins University (although he eventually dropped out), Sally S. graduated from a women's college, Edward F. got a degree in history, Clarence B. got a B.A. from a college in Illinois and Fred G. was "doing well at university".

There are several well-known cases (such as Temple Grandin) of people diagnosed with autism in childhood who have gone on to get PhDs – recently, Therese Joliffe (at the University of Cambridge in the UK) became the first person with autism to get a PhD for research into autism.

For many people, university was the first chance they had had to experience formal education as enjoyable and to discover themselves as competent. Universities were often much more suited to the learning style of people with Asperger's:

> In community college, I began to experience myself as a smart person fully for the first time. The high school daily schedule of 6 class periods in one day just didn't fit my learning style. The flexibility of a college schedule did … I transferred after two years to a small private university. There the process of discovering that I wasn't stupid, just learned differently continued. (Karen)

> Well, the first thing was that I could have my own mind about something … and I could get extensions on essays and I was able to get more involved with classes at my own pace. [The] tutor for the health and social psychology courses I did told me she'd seen me blossom … What helped was being treated with respect and – if I made mistakes – being corrected in a more positive way than happened at school … constructive criticism … (David A.)

University qualifications can help make someone employable, and the behaviour of someone with Asperger's syndrome is often much more readily tolerated when it comes from someone academic, fitting into the stereotype of the "eccentric professor". Peers often became more accepting, too, as they moved out of the social intolerance typical of teenagers. The social and practical aspects of the environment still remain the most challenging: coping with shared accommodation, remembering to eat and to have occasional baths, for example, can all turn into major problems.

Clearly, schools should not be too quick to rule out university as a possibility and, where someone's academic abilities make it an option, it needs to be taken into account in planning from much earlier on – for example, making sure that they gain the necessary qualifications for university entrance. This is why I have covered the topic in disproportionate detail here.

Obviously, university will not be a possibility for many people with Asperger's, but further education and training of all sorts can be equally useful in providing room for continued development and learning while hopefully gaining qualifications. Local community colleges can be helpful for people who are still living at home and, like university, can provide a first chance to enjoy learning, to choosing courses and specialize in areas of strength.

Like schools, both further and higher educational establishments are unlikely to have much knowledge of Asperger's syndrome, and so many of the same problems can arise. A strong support network and a mentor of some sort who can provide advice and, advocacy if necessary, are indispensable. The INTERACT Centre in London is unique in providing further education specifically for people with Asperger's syndrome.

Unemployment is a significant problem even among the most over-qualified people with Asperger's syndrome. While we may have no problem with the actual work involved in a given job, the social skills necessary to pass an interview and to get by in the workplace without evoking hostility and rejection from workmates may be beyond us. The successful jobs tend to be those which provide a niche for someone with a particular specialized talent and in which the demand for interaction with others is very limited.

I have tried very briefly to sketch some of the issues involved in further/higher education and employment for people with Asperger's syndrome; each could quite easily take up a book of its own. What I have tried to do is provide enough of a "taster" to get teachers and other professionals to start thinking about the future of their pupils and what awaits them when they leave school. It is vital to start thinking and planning while a child is still at school if proper preparation for the transition is to be in place by the time they leave.

9

Talking about asperger's syndrome

> I tried asking questions to find out if there was anything tangibly the matter with me. I had this vague, insistent idea all the time – that there was something wrong with me. But questions that to me were deeply serious were answered in amused voices: 'Oh, no, there's nothing wrong with you, dear.' (Gerland 1997, p. 127)

People lie to children with Asperger's syndrome; there is no other way of putting it. All of us grow up hearing variants on the following from everyone around us:

Everybody feels like that sometimes.

You can do it if you just try.

I'm sure they like you really.

It's just friendly teasing.

Just be yourself and everything will be fine.

There's nothing the matter with you.

Obviously, any of these statements may be true in a given situation, but they are usually made by adults on the basis of no evidence at all or in blatant contradiction of the facts as reported by the child. They are intended to reassure and comfort, but the effect of such "reassurance" is often the opposite: the child is left wondering: if everybody feels like this, why am I the only one who can't cope? If everybody likes me, why do they not want to talk to me? If I'm supposed to "just be myself", why does it always get me into trouble?

Because of our great difficulties in deciphering the social world by ourselves, we are particularly dependent on receiving accurate information from adults. When adults lie, out of a desire to avoid harsh truths, they end up "gaslighting" us – undermining our ability to trust our own observations and judgements and convincing us that our correct perceptions are delusional. It is not surprising that many of us end up believing that we are crazy.

Clearly, parents will feel that it is up to them to decide how and when a child should be told, but teachers and other professionals can play a vital role in advising parents on why it is important to explain Asperger's syndrome to their children and how this can best be done.

Sometimes people decide that they will not broach the subject until the child spontaneously starts to ask about it; this seriously underestimates the degree to which children, especially children with Asperger's, can worry about a topic without approaching their parents about it, and, as Gunilla Gerland (2000b) writes, "...how difficult it is to ask about something which you don't have words for."

Any child with Asperger's who is old enough to understand a simple verbal explanation of their condition is also old enough, if they don't get such an explanation, to notice that they are different from their "normal" peers, and that they have difficulty doing things which seem to be easy for "normal" children. Often they will infer that there must be something wrong with them. Many people with Asperger's concluded as children that they must be "stupid", "crazy" "retarded", "brain-damaged" or that what was wrong with them must be so awful that no-one would talk about it. I alternated between believing that, because my experiences and feelings were so different from everyone else's, I must have incipient schizophrenia and that it was only a matter of time before I disintegrated completely and, convincing myself that, just as everyone kept telling me, there was nothing wrong with me and I could be like everyone else if only I tried harder (I must just not be trying hard enough). The fear and misery that this caused should be easy to imagine.

Simply not knowing why, for example, certain noises upset you, can be frightening and frustrating in itself. As Gunilla Gerland, who has worked extensively with professionals and schools on how to talk about Asperger's syndrome to children with Asperger's, points out, "These situations where you suddenly realise you can't do something which is very easy to other people, *and you have no idea why you can't do it*, are very frustrating … just to be able to explain to yourself why you can't do some things is very helpful." (Gerland, 2000b)

A label is the key to self-understanding. A label lets a child know that their disability is not their fault; it lets them know that their problem has a name; and it lets them know that there are others out there like them.

Accurate self-understanding is vital if a child is to take control and learn how to manage and work around their problems and make the best use of their strengths. Gerland comments on how learning about Asperger's seems to help children reflect on their own behaviour and problems, often for the first time in their lives: "they suddenly start discussing spontaneously ... what fits the description of them." (Gerland, 2000b)

Becoming aware of how one functions and of how others may perceive one's behaviour is essential if a child is to be able to begin to develop their own creative solutions to the problems they may come across, instead of being perpetually dependent on others for help. Knowledge, as Francis Bacon pointed out, is power.

It's important to be positive and not to paint a picture of Asperger's syndrome as a "disease" or simply as something that prevents you from doing what you want to do, but it's also important not to deny the real difficulties that can be involved. Only when it has been acknowledged that a child is genuinely different from others and does have problems is it possible to go on to build a positive self-image based on acceptance and even celebration of differences.

For many people, like me, getting a diagnosis of Asperger's is a huge relief. Elizabeth reported that, on finding out about Asperger's syndrome, she felt: "Like Einstein must have felt when he discovered relativity! Suddenly everything is logical and makes sense! "

For others, though, the diagnosis can be hard to come to terms with:

> I didn't want anything to do with it. It scared me. I didn't like going to the psychologists and eventually just stopped going – I was obviously free to do so and they didn't bother me again. (David Hawker)

Some will refuse to listen to or read anything about Asperger's syndrome, or even consider the possibility that they could have it. For people who had been led to hope that one day they would manage to "try hard enough" and all their problems would go away, leaving them "normal", a formal diagnosis can mean the end of those hopes and a consequent need to mourn. Some are also painfully aware of the stigma attached to having a "psychiatric" condition.

This doesn't mean that information should be withheld. In almost all cases, the news of a diagnosis takes a long time to absorb, and those breaking the news should not expect the reaction (whether of relief, grief, or a mixture of both) to be immediate, or take the initial reaction to be all there is to someone's response (instead of the beginning of the process of digesting the news). Even when a reaction is positive, it may still be a long time before that person decides that they would like, for example, to meet other people with Asperger's syndrome. It is best to make such opportunities available, but to allow the person to find their own pace and not push them into anything before they feel ready.

Often it can be helpful to have some written material on Asperger's that the child or young person can refer to in private. Booklets aimed specifically at children and young people with Asperger's, like Gunilla Gerland's *Finding Out About Asperger Syndrome, High Functioning Autism and PDD* (2000), can be invaluable.

It is important not to give the impression that everything about Asperger's syndrome is known, or that one knows the child better than they know themselves, but to recognize and help a child to articulate their own knowledge of how they function – to empower them to become experts on their own condition. As Gerland points out:

> … *you are not best helped if the people around you … act as experts telling you that they know exactly what your condition is. What you need is guiding from them to come to your own truth, and to develop your personal approach to your condition. (Gerland, 2000b)*

10
Conclusion

Don't assume you know what the child is like if you have read a manual about autism. There are as many brands of autism as there are autistic people. Look and listen to the individual person ... (Darius)

Reading about Asperger's syndrome is indispensable, but it should be the starting point for teachers working with schoolchildren with Asperger's, not the finishing point. I have tried to describe how I and others experienced school in the hope that it will enable teachers to approach schoolchildren with Asperger's syndrome with greater understanding and insight but this cannot be done without willingness to question all prior assumptions (including any derived from this book) and to listen to the children themselves. Many will share the experiences and problems I have described but not all will share all of them. Each child with Asperger's is an individual. Some, if asked, will be able to articulate for themselves what they need in order to learn and how they would like school to be different. Others will not and it will be up to their teachers to listen to the messages communicated through their behaviour.

Schoolchildren with Asperger's syndrome are clearly not the easiest pupils to have in one's class, and even those who are most sympathetic to us seem to find us baffling and even infuriating at times. Nevertheless, I hope I can say without boasting that we must also be among the most interesting and challenging students that a teacher will ever encounter.

We also offer teachers that rare thing: the chance to make a real difference. One point that stood out from many different stories was that the presence of even one teacher who was willing to approach a student with Asperger's with insight and respect could make a dramatic difference to the whole of their school career and even to their life as a whole (even though that student might not have been able to express their gratitude or provide any positive feedback at the time). Conversely, ignorance and intolerance could scar a child for life.

I cannot think of a better way to end this book than to repeat what Hans Asperger wrote more than fifty years ago when he first described the children who came to be described as having "Asperger's syndrome" (1991 p. 90):

> … that the knowledge of the great range of possible outcomes and the clear dependence of outcome on the quality of education received 'gives us the right and the duty to speak out for such children with the whole force of our personality.'

Appendix A: Recommended Reading

These books represent a very small fraction of the vast number about autism and Asperger's syndrome and there are many others which I personally have enjoyed and learnt from. However, I feel that these particular books would be especially valuable to any teacher or other professional working with a schoolchild with Asperger's and would be ideal complements to this one.

Attwood, Tony (1997), Asperger's Syndrome: *A Guide for Parents and Professionals*, Jessica Kingsley Publishers, London.

> This is a very clear and sympathetic book which many people with Asperger's agree is particularly insightful.

Cumine, Val, Leach, Julia & Stevenson, Gill (1998), *Asperger Syndrome: A Practical Guide for Teachers*, David Fulton Publishers, London.

> A concise and practical guide for teachers.

Gerland, Gunilla (1997), *A Real Person: Life on the Outside*, Souvenir Press, London.

> This autobiography about growing up with undiagnosed Asperger's is the best first-person account that I've read and describes school experiences with particular eloquence and force.

Greene, Ross W. (1998), *The Explosive Child: A New Approach for Understanding and Parenting Easily Frustrated, 'Chronically Inflexible' Children*, HarperCollins Publishers, New York.

> This isn't specifically about kids with Asperger's but describes a specific pattern of "challenging behaviour" displayed by many children and young people with Asperger's. Greene gives practical advice on how

to cope in the short-term and how to develop a child's flexibility and coping skills in the long-term.

Howlin, Patricia (1997), *Autism: Preparing for Adulthood*, Routledge, London.

This focuses specifically on issues facing adolescents and young adults on the autistic spectrum, especially the more high-functioning. Even if the children you are working with are younger, it's vital to look ahead and start preparing.

McDonnell, Jane Taylor (with an afterword by Paul McDonnell) (1993), *News From the Border: A Mother's Memoir of Her Autistic Son*, Ticknor and Fields, New York.

This sensitive and painfully honest account of bringing up a son with high-functioning autism/Asperger's syndrome illuminates the reasons why young people with Asperger's are so vulnerable to anxiety and depression and the considerable stresses and strains upon their parents.

Sinclair, Jim (1993) "Don't Mourn For Us", http://www.autreat.com/dont_mourn.html

This famous essay, aimed primarily at parents, challenges the idea of autism as a "tragedy". It has spurred many people to re-assess their perceptions of autistic spectrum conditions and the way in which they work with, and relate to, people with autism and Asperger's.

Appendix B:
Resources

The central resource for information and support concerning Asperger's syndrome in the UK is the National Autistic Society, who also publish a newsletter, *Asperger United*, by and for people with Asperger's.

> The National Autistic Society
> 393 City Road
> London EC1V 1NG
> Helpline: 0845 070 4004
> Tel: +44 (0)20 7833 2299; Fax: +44 (0)20 7833 9666
> Email: nas@nas.org.uk
> Website: http://www.nas.org.uk

The NAS run a specialist centre for diagnosis of autism and Asperger's syndrome which is a national centre of expertise:

> The Centre for Social and Communication Disorders
> Elliot House
> 113 Masons Hill
> Bromley
> Kent BR2 9HT
> Tel: 020 8466 0098
> Fax: 020 8466 0118
> Email: elliot.house@nas.org.uk
> Website: http://www.patient.co.uk

> The INTERACT Centre
> c/o Hanwell Community Centre
> Westcott Crescent
> London W7 1PD
> Website: http://www.interactcenter.com
> A specialist further education college for people with Asperger's syndrome.

As I have noted, information on the internet is not always reliable, balanced or helpful; however, the Online Asperger Syndrome Information and Support site (OASIS) at http://www.udel.edu/bkirby/asperger is a welcome exception, combining original articles, papers (including a lot of information specifically on educational issues) and bulletin boards with links to pretty much all reliable material on the internet concerning Asperger's. As a "first stop" for on-line information on Asperger's, it is unrivalled.

The Autism Picture Page at http://www.linds.net constructed by Lindsay Weekes, who has high-functioning autism, is a wonderful site of photographs of people with autistic spectrum conditions, from Asperger's syndrome to severe autism, with "inside" explanations of the behaviours shown. Divided into sections with themes such as "Absorption" and "Caution", it is invaluable for anyone who wants to get a feel for autistic ways of perceiving and responding to the world.

Bibliography

American Psychiatric Association (1994), *Desk Reference to the Diagnostic Criteria from DSM-IV*, Washington DC.

Asperger, Hans (1991), "'Autistic psychopathy' in childhood", translated and annotated by Uta Frith, in Frith, Uta, (ed.) *Autism and Asperger's Syndrome*, Cambridge University Press, Cambridge, pp. 37–92.

Attwood, Tony (1997), *Asperger's Syndrome: A Guide for Parents and Professionals*, Jessica Kingsley, London.

Attwood, Tony (not dated), "Asperger Syndrome: Some Common Questions", http://www.asperger.org/articles/asp000.asp

Autisme-Europe (1998), Code of Good Practice on Prevention of Violence Against Persons with Autism, Bruxelles, Belgium.

Bauer, Stephen (not dated), "Asperger Syndrome", http://www.asperger.org/articles/asp000.asp

Bishop, Dorothy (1989), "Autism, Asperger's syndrome and semantic-pragmatic disorder: Where are the boundaries?", http://www.mugsy.org/bishop.htm

Brown, Hilary, and Smith, Helen (eds.) (1992), *Normalisation: A Reader for the Nineties*, Routledge, London.

Cohen, Leah Hager (1995), *Train Go Sorry: Inside A DeafWorld*, Vintage Books, New York.

Connor, Michael (1999), "Asperger Syndrome (Autistic Spectrum Disorder) and the Self-Reports of Comprehensive School Students", http://www.mugsy.org/connor15.htm

Cumine, Val, Leach, Julia and Stevenson, Gill (1998), *Asperger Syndrome: A Practical Guide for Teachers*, David Fulton Publishers, London.

DfEE (1995), The National Curriculum, http://www.dfee.gov.uk/nc/

Edelson, Meredyth Goldberg (1995), "Social Stories", http://www.autism.org/stories.html

Frith, Uta (1989), *Autism: Explaining the Enigma*, Blackwell, Oxford.

Frith, Uta (ed.) (1991), *Autism and Asperger's Syndrome*, Cambridge University Press, Cambridge.

Frith, Uta and Happé, Francesca (1994) 'Autism: Beyond theory of mind', *Cognition*, 50 (1994), pp. 115–132.

Gerland, Gunilla (1997), *A Real Person: Life on the Outside*, trans Joan Tate, Souvenir Press, London.

Gerland, Gunilla (2000a), *Finding Out About Asperger Syndrome, High Functioning Autism and PDD*, Jessica Kingsley Publishers, London.

Gerland, Gunilla (2000b), "Normality vs. Self Esteem: The Road to Increased Independence and Reflective Thinking in Children and Young Persons with AS/HFA", presentation at Autism-Europe Congress 2000, Glasgow.

Grandin, Temple, and Scariano, Margaret (1993), *Emergence: Labeled Autistic*, Arena Press, Novato, CA.

Grandin, Temple (1995), *Thinking in Pictures: and other reports from my life with autism*, Doubleday, New York.

Grandin, Temple (revised 1996), "Making the Transition from the World of School into the World of Work" http://www.autism.org//temple/transition.html

Grandin, Temple (1998), "Teaching Tips for Children and Adults with Autism", http://www.autism.org//temple/tips.html

Greene, Ross W. (1998), *The Explosive Child: A New Approach for Understanding and Parenting Easily Frustrated, 'Chronically Inflexible' Children*, Harper Collins, New York.

Howlin, Patricia (1997), *Autism: Preparing for Adulthood*, Routledge, London.

Howlin, Patricia (1998), *Children with Autism and Asperger Syndrome: A Guide for Practitioners and Carers*, John Wiley and Sons, Chichester.

Jackel, Susan (1996), "Asperger's Syndrome – Educational Management Issues", http://www.udel.edu/bkirby/asperger/education.html

Jolliffe, Therese (1992), Lansdowne, Richard, and Robinson, Clive, "Autism: a Personal Account", *Communication*, Vol. 26 (3), December.

Jordan, Rita and Powell, Stuart (1995), *Understanding and Teaching Children with Autism*, John Wiley and Sons, Chichester.

Kanner, Leo (1973), "How Far Can Autistic Children Go in Matters of Social Adaptation?", in Kanner (ed.) *Childhood Psychosis: Initial Studies and New Insights*, V.H. Winston and Sons, Washington DC, pp. 189–214.

Kauffman, James M., and Hallahan, Daniel P. (eds.) (1995), *The Illusion of Full Inclusion: A Comprehensive Critique of a Current Special Education Bandwagon*, PRO-ED, Inc., Austin, TX.

Lawson, Wendy (1998), *Life Behind Glass: A Personal Account of Autistic Spectrum Disorder*, Southern Cross University Press, Lismore, NSW.

Lawson, Wendy (1999), "Adolescents, Autism Spectrum Disorder And Secondary School", http://www.mugsy.org/wendy/asschool.htm

McDonnell, Jane Taylor and McDonnell, Paul (1993), *News From The Border: A Mother's Memoir of Her Autistic Son*, Ticknor & Fields, New York.

Mesibov, Gary, and Shea, Victoria (not dated), "The Culture of Autism: From Theoretical Understanding to Educational Practice", http://www.autismuk.com/index3sub1.htm

Moreno, Susan, and O'Neal, Carol, "Tips For Teaching High Functioning People With Autism", http://www.udel.edu/bkirby/asperger/education.html

Opie, Iona and Peter, Opie (1959), *The Lore and Language of Schoolchildren*, Oxford University Press, London.

Peeters, Theo, and Gillberg, Christopher (1999), *Autism: Medical and Educational Aspects*, second edition, Whurr Publishers, London.

Roberts, Jeannie (1995), *Dear Psychiatrist ... : Do Child Care Specialists Understand?*, The Lutterworth Press, Cambridge.

Robinson, George, and Maines, Barbara (1997), *Crying For Help: the No Blame Approach to Bullying*, Lucky Duck Publishing, Bristol.

Saskatchewan Education Special Education Unit (not dated), "Educating The Student With Asperger Syndrome", http://www.sasked.gov.sk.ca/curr_inst/speced/asper.html

Schopler, Eric (ed.) (1998), *Asperger Syndrome or High-Functioning Autism?*, Plenum Publishers, New York.

Shields, Jane (not dated), "Semantic Pragmatic Impairments Information Sheet", http://www.mugsy.org/spd5.htm

Sinclair, Jim (1993), "Don't Mourn For Us", http://members.xoom.com/JimSinclair/dontmourn.htm

Sinclair, Jim, (1998), "Concerns about inclusion from within the disability community", http://members.xoom.com/JimSinclair/inclusion.htm

Sinclair, Jim (1999), "Why I dislike 'person first' language", http://members.xoom.com/JimSinclair/person_first.htm

Solursh, Susan T. (1999) "The relation between adult outcome and parental acceptance of autism/PDD during childhood", unpublished study performed for Master of Applied Science degree, University of Waterloo, Waterloo, Canada.

Szivos, Sue (1992), "The limits of integration?", in Hilary Brown and Helen Smith (eds), *Normalisation: A Reader for the Nineties*, pp. 112–133, Routledge, London.

Tucker, Elly (ed.) "Asperger's Syndrome Guide for Teachers", http://www.udel.edu/bkirby/asperger/education.html

Williams, Karen (not dated), "Understanding the Student With Asperger's Syndrome: Guidelines for Teachers", http://www.udel.edu/bkirby/asperger/education.html

Wing, Lorna (1981), "Asperger syndrome: a clinical account", http://www.mugsy.org/wing2.htm

Wolff, Sula (1995), *Loners: The Life Path of Unusual Children*, Routledge, London.